THE BIORHYTHM
LIFE PLANNER

THE BIORHYTHM LIFE PLANNER

HOW TO PLAN YOUR LIFE FOR PEAK PERFORMANCE

Peter Gotzl
Andrew Happe
Paul Schenk

Thorsons
An Imprint of HarperCollins*Publishers*

Thorsons
An imprint of HarperCollinsPublishers
77-85 Fulham Palace Road
Hammersmith, London W6 8JB

Published by Thorsons 1991

10 9 8 7 6 5 4 3 2 1

A catalogue record for this book
is available from the British Library

ISBN 0 7225 2515 X

Printed in Great Britain by
The Bath Press, Bath, Avon

CONTENTS

This book is dedicated to the memory of
Vera Norman who had such faith in our ability
to develop and extend the boundaries of biorhythm.

INTRODUCTION

Within all of us there are many different cycles and rhythms that control the functions of the body; most of them are not totally regular, and will vary from person to person. However, three particular cycles do exist that influence our physical, emotional and intellectual capacities on a very regular and predictable basis. These three rhythms are collectively known as biorhythm.

During the early part of this century three independent European researchers were drawn to the fact that people seemed to be affected by consistent repeating rhythms, and over a period of years their work has formed the basis of the science of biorhythm. The three cycles that make up a person's biorhythm are the 23-day physical cycle, the 28-day emotional cycle and the 33-day intellectual cycle. All these cycles begin at the moment we are born and continue to repeat themselves with total accuracy for the rest of our lives. Biorhythm is a science that can be used in many areas of life to improve the way we perform, not only on a personal basis but also the way that we interact with other people in relationships – personal and professional.

This book is the total guide to biorhythm and it enables you to apply the science for yourself, without the need for complicated calculations, by employing a simple and effective way to actually set up your own biorhythm positions with our patented transparent overlay technique. A simple set of tables and the ingenious biorhythm display system enables you to calculate and display your own biorhythm positions in under two minutes.

Biorhythm is now widely used all over the world, being especially popular in Japan and America where people and companies are applying the science to reduce accident rates, improve relationships and to simply get the best out of themselves. The science has its critics, but a huge amount of research and investigation has taken place by many recognised organisations over the last 40 years that have produced astonishing results. It is still not clear what actually causes this phenomenon to operate in the way that it does but for most people this is not as important as the fact that the science does actually work.

Our involvement with the science of biorhythm is not limited to the production of this book; we are also heavily involved in many other biorhythm projects that are all intended to make the adoption of the science easier and more effective for the people that are interested. The World Biorhythm Club is the hub of our operation and is based in Oxford, England, where we are developing and installing advanced computer biorhythm systems into shops and retail outlets. The reason that Biorhythm is not as commercially popular as subjects such as astrology lies very much in the fact that insufficient advances have been made in reducing the complexity of the science for people effectively to be able to follow it without having to constantly make calculations and draw a mental picture of their Biorhythm positions – Biorhythm is a very visual science and needs to be treated as one.

We are always interested to hear of any research or discoveries that people or organisations have made on this subject and we are happy to help out in any projects that may be taking place. Biorhythm can open many areas of previously locked potential to those who wish to benefit from its power and the *Biorhythm Life Planner* should be used as a tool to help you realise your own goals.

THE WORLD BIORHYTHM CLUB,
33 West Way,
Oxford,
England,
OX2 OJE

1

THE BIORHYTHM STORY

Biorhythm can be traced back to the turn of the century, when early research work began to reveal that certain people under professional medical observation displayed characteristic and repeating 'rhythms' that could affect the way they felt and performed on certain days. It was understood from an early stage that these rhythms were not random in their activity, and perhaps could explain why all people encounter ever-changing biological periods, e.g. when their resistance to disease or ability to perform physical tasks will show a large variation. The real significance of this discovery, however, was that while many recognised researchers were already aware of the existence of this phenomenon they did not as yet have a proven method of actually calculating when these periods would be likely to occur, nor a scientific framework with which to test and develop their theories. With the arrival of biorhythm they were now able to calculate, with extreme accuracy, those times during our lives when we will encounter such periods, also giving them a suitably credible theory with which to expand their research into the wider scientific community.

The science of biorhythm evolved from the work that was originally carried out by three eminent European doctors in the early part of this century. Dr Hermann Swoboda was a professor of Psychology at the University of Vienna and as a result of the work that he was carrying out with his patients he became drawn to the fact that rhythms seemed to exist which influenced the way his patients felt about themselves, influenced their creative ability and also affected their dream patterns. He investigated the way in which the body seemed to be more susceptible to infections and poor periods of health at certain times than at others. Swoboda continued with total fascination to research biorhythm alongside the duties he performed as a professor at the University, producing numerous publications that detailed his work, including establishing the now accepted fact that the body had two definite rhythms which affect it on an extremely accurate and regular basis. These were the 23-day physical and 28-day emotional rhythms.

Swoboda's success with biorhythm can be attributed largely to the fact that he was an intense researcher, his detailing and analysis of data gave him an excellent database to work from. Swoboda began his work with biorhythm in the late 1890s influenced by reports and papers that he read which referred to the altered mental states and psychological variations in human behaviour. The suggestions that these reports were making and the fact that they could not provide any sound basis for explanation sparked off what was to become a new area of research and discovery for Swoboda. Swoboda's involvement with biorhythm was to continue until 1954.

During the course of his research Swoboda looked at many areas of medicine that were at the time fairly unexplored as he tried to find links with biorhythm. One area of research that interested him greatly was whether there was an inherited link that was transferred from generation to generation, whether the timing of birth could be associated with biorhythm. It was this type of heightened and comprehensive study of the human 'machine' that led to Swoboda being taken very seriously in recognised fields of intellectual excellence. Swoboda also realised soon after he had started his work with biorhythm that a method, other than the tedious mathematical calculations, needed to be found to calculate critical days and general biorhythm positions. The need to find an alternative method was important for two reasons. First, it would enable him to work faster and with more accuracy, and secondly, it was important that people who wanted to examine his findings had a method of doing so that didn't require the same level of involvement that he was applying.

In 1909 Swoboda developed what was almost certainly the first biorhythm calculator for the 23- and 28-day cycles. Swoboda devised a slide rule calculator that enabled people to calculate critical days. Of the many publications that Swoboda produced relating to biorhythm there was one that stood out from the rest. *The Year of Seven* was published towards the end of his writing career and was a 600-page study that looked at the effect of biorhythm within the family structure. As Swoboda had satisfied himself that there was a connection between biorhythm and an individual's many shifts in physical and mental performance, he decided to explore the boundaries of the science further. Many of the common death causes were studied to see if there was a genetic link between biorhythm and the blood line of the family. Swoboda concluded in his findings that the events which he had analysed did actually show a periodic tendency.

Dr Hermann Swoboda was recognised for his work with Biorhythm both by the city of Vienna and the University to which he had devoted much of his life. By the time of his death at the age of ninety in 1963, this man with such a passion for discovery had been able to witness the largescale acceptance of his biorhythm theory across the world.

During the same period Dr Wilhelm Fleiss, who was later to become the President of the German Academy of Sciences, was also working – totally independently of Swoboda – on a theory that followed strikingly similar lines. Fleiss was a practising doctor when he first became interested in the patterns or rhythms he was finding in patients. It seemed to him that they were influencing the ability of his patients to respond to treatment. Quite simply, the treatments that he prescribed did not always have the same effect. Fleiss worked primarily with children to try to determine why some of them seemed to have a strong resistance to infections and disease while others who were exposed to the source of the infection at the same time did not. Data was collected and analysed over a number of years which, when set down in a more formal and mathematical manner, showed that he had arrived at exactly the same point as Swoboda, in that he believed the body was affected by these two 23- and 28-day cycles.

Although Fleiss was a successful man he was never really able to achieve the same level of recognition for his work with biorhythm as Swoboda had. The people of Berlin, where he was based, found his methods to be complicated and cumbersome. He was faced with the same problems as Swoboda: the mathematical complexities of demonstrating and even calculating his findings. These were days long before calculators and computers and the only way of analysing data was with pen and paper and a certain amount of mathematical flair. Fleiss had to enrol the aid of a mathematician to assist him in producing his findings.

Fleiss continued his extensive research into the science, going down many of the same paths as Swoboda had done, and produced a number of publications that arrived at similar conclusions to those of his counterpart. He also conducted lectures on the subject and made available calculation tables to enable people to utilise the science. Unfortunately he was never really able to communicate his findings in a simple enough manner to see his work with the science accepted on such a large scale. His death in 1928 came quite a few years before Berlin realised the importance of his discovery. It should be noted, however, that his work with biorhythm was as fundamental in terms of acceptance as the work that Swoboda had carried out. The significance of two such eminent men arriving at almost identical conclusions, independently of each other, should not be overlooked during this historical period of discovery.

Biorhythm went on to become the study of three cycles when further research that was being carried out in the late 1920s became available. In the town of Innsbruck in Austria an engineer named Alfred Teltscher was conducting research into a cycle that he believed he had identified. Teltscher had decided to try to evaluate whether the academic performance of students was influenced by a cyclical rhythm, and his research was centred around the analysis of students' results in pre-set examinations to see if there was a definite pattern that could be linked to a regular cycle. He found that there was indeed a discernable pattern, a 33-day cycle seemed to be in operation that affected the performance of students under a testing/stressful situation.

This discovery answered a question that had been with him for some years, namely why there could often be a noticeable variation in the standard of work that he was witnessing in certain individual students. He was intrigued by the fact that often a student would perform at below par for no apparent reason. The careful analysis of many schoolchildren as well as his own students provided him with the information that he required to explore the subject fully. He compiled the information and set about looking for a cycle length that would hopefully correlate with the data that he had before him. His arrival at the 33-day cycle could really best be explained as a matter of deduction because if the cycle existed at all then it was of course only a matter of time before he discovered it.

The work of Teltscher was not as advanced and comprehensive as that of Swoboda and Fleiss but nevertheless it completed the overall biorhythm formula that we are familiar with today. It is the findings of these three pioneers that have led to the eventual acceptance of biorhythm as a science which holds many answers to previously unanswerable questions on human behavioural patterns.

Biorhythm has been put to a number of serious uses over the last few years, some of the most important being to improve efficiency and reduce accident rates in industry. In Japan, the popularity of biorhythm is very evident with a number of nationally organised biorhythm associations. The 'big three' are based in Tokyo and they are the Nihon Biorhythm Institute, the Tokai Biorhythm Centre and the Nihon Biorhythm Association.

BIORHYTHM APPLICATION AND USES

Japan's interest in the science has almost certainly stemmed from the fact that it is something which can offer them a way of improving their competitive performance in many fields of activity, without the need for costly investment. The introduction of biorhythm to Japan can be traced back to 1965 when a book published on the subject prompted a leading Professor at the Institute of Public Health in Tokyo, Mr Kichinosuke Tatai, to examine the science further. The interest in the science then grew quickly as the marketing flair and promotional skills of Tatai generated new areas of application. Interest in the science spread through to industry and over the years biorhythm was adopted by a large number of companies to help reduce their accident rates. A number of world leaders were using the science as long ago as the late 1960s: companies such as Mitsubishi, Fuji, and Hitachi to name a few. The adoption of biorhythm spread to almost all activities of commercial life with many of the larger insurance companies offering their customers personalised biorhythm information in an attempt to attract business and of course reduce the accident rates.

Many of the Japanese transport companies also got involved with the science as they recognised the potential advantages it was able to offer, especially in reducing the ever-increasing number of accidents. The success that these companies achieved has been well documented in many reports and can only really be described as astounding. Prior to the introduction of biorhythm, accident rates were often calculated and checks were carried out to establish whether there was a direct correlation between them and the biorhythm condition of the individual concerned. Many of the studies that took place demonstrated that the accidents occurred with a much higher than normal frequency on the critical day. This was not just a small swing but a correlation that left little doubt in the researchers' minds that the effects of the critical day were certainly not to be underestimated.

Some of the best documented studies from Japan come from a selection of large companies but the list is very long and most cases are equally impressive. The Ohmi Railway company operated a fleet of buses and taxis in Japan and carried out a very detailed study between 1963 and 1969. They found that 59 per cent of their accidents during this period occurred during the drivers' critical days. This figure was over twice the statistical likelihood and as a result led to implementation of a biorhythm strategy. The basic method that was employed was to issue any driver with a critical day a warning card that reminded him that extra care was required during that day. If it sounds too simple to be true, one should take note that over the next four years the company's accident rate fell by over 50 per cent, despite a 40 per cent increase in the number of miles covered, all of which was against a background of increased motor vehicle traffic on the roads.

In 1971 the Tokyo Metropolitan Police produced a report that detailed traffic accidents that had occurred as a result of driver error the previous year. Their findings were that 70 per cent of these had occurred on the drivers' critical days, and the report also included statistics on pedestrian accidents which showed a quite remarkable 80 per cent correlation. These results do seem a bit too good, but even allowing for the possibility of some information errors, there is strong evidence here that the critical day has some form of 'magnetic' effect in terms of attracting accidents. The Tokyo police were not the only police force to study biorhythm. The Osaka police carried out similar tests on child pedestrians, and their results showed that over 70 per cent of accidents that occurred as a direct result of the child being at fault, occurred on the child's critical day. As a result of this type of study many accident prevention programmes were initiated in Japan using the positive benefits that biorhythm knowledge was able to offer. The accident rates in those areas using this type of preventative action dropped substantially. Similar studies have been carried out in Europe and more often than not the results have been very conclusive and supportive.

Most of this type of research can only be traced back to the period between the late 1950s and the early 1970s. Why this should be so is difficult to say, as it does seem strange that biorhythm has gone relatively quiet in the last twenty years. Of course there have been a few studies that have failed to produce any connection between the critical day and accident rates, but there are a number of reasons which could have caused this seeming biorhythm failure. To start with, the nature of the accident as well as the accurate interpretation of the data at hand is essential if biorhythm is to offer any conclusive evidence. Some of the results that have been found are so spectacular it is natural that the science would be questioned for feasibility. Who can honestly say they would immediately believe in the possibility that a particular, cyclically repeating day which we all continually experience during our lives, is over three times as likely to attract a self-caused accident than any other day? The only way to find out for yourself is to do some research of your own. Finding the data for this type of exercise is very easy from our own experiences, e.g. when did I last bump the car? But beware, the results that you may achieve could easily change the way you deal with life.

A number of airline accidents have been investigated with the use of biorhythm and here also the critical day factor has been found to influence pilot performance. In many cases of pilot error the critical day occurrence has been found to be far higher than statistically expected. This type of research almost certainly led airlines such as United Airlines and Swissair to consider the implementation of biorhythm as something that could offer safety benefits. Swissair incorporated biorhythm into the scheduling of pilot rotas to try to ensure that no two pilots that had a critical day at the same time flew together. This type of policy demonstrated their belief in the science. United Airlines used biorhythm in a different way by applying it to their ground staff in 1973. The results were effective with a large reduction in the accident rate of workers and technicians and the consequent benefits of fewer lost working days.

The ways that the science can be applied are almost endless as there are so many applications that it can be used for, from the business world through to just using it as a fun and interesting pastime, but in order to get the best out of biorhythm there has to be a practical and quick way to calculate and display the conditions. Since the subject of biorhythm began to enjoy popularity there have been many different options available to the enthusiast, some good and some not so good. For example, a number of personal computers available today come complete with a biorhythm programme that the operator can run to display condition cycles. While this type of presentation is accurate it is lacking graphical display quality, and also these systems do not carry any form of personalised explanation with them. Casio, the well-known Japanese electronics company, produce a biorhythm watch and also a biorhythm calculator which calculate your daily positions in each of the three cycles; however, they do not display the pattern of your cycles. A few fairly complex slide rule calculators are also in existence that can again indicate where you are in each of your cycles, but do not offer any sort of ongoing practical advice.

Some of the books that have been published on this subject have also tried to make the setting of your biorhythm simple and quick but these systems have actually been very complicated and time consuming and often required the person to actually draw their own biorhythm curves on a separate piece of paper, which is hardly what could be termed either accurate or practical.

For biorhythm to be something that holds your interest the matter of easy use is a very important one. Like most things in life, the easier they are to apply and understand the more likely you are to follow them with any sort of commitment. The method that we have designed for the purpose of this book is what we believe to be the fastest and easiest and yet still 100 per cent accurate way to set your, or indeed anybody else's biorhythm condition.

A common question is why the science of biorhythm is

nowhere near as popular as, for instance, astrology and why there is only a relatively small amount of material available on the subject. We think that the reason for this lies in the fact that there simply have not been any really innovative yet practical methods for the general public to apply the science to themselves. Another reason is that biorhythm is far more personalised than general astrology which places individuals in one of 12 categories, the zodiac signs. For this reason it is easy and practical to run 'your stars' in newspapers. If you wanted to run a biorhythm phase table in a newspaper the exercise would be far more complicated. The problem with this would be that while there are only really 27 main permutations that exist between the three cycles, the calculation that is required to find which phase you are in would have to be done by the individual concerned and could not be done by the newspaper. Accordingly, for something to catch on in the commercial sense, it is usually a prerequisite that the consumer does not have to put any effort or thought into the service that is being provided for them. This is really the main failing of the science, and it is sad but unfortunately true that most people are not willing to get involved in biorhythm because it seems too complicated to set up. The truth is of course that biorhythm is very simple in theory and only requires a basic understanding in order to be applied effectively. While it cannot be painted quite as simply as astrology, it does have far more to offer including a very scientific and well-tested background.

If we are to see this subject enjoy the popularity that it deserves then there are a number of things that will have to change. Since the completion of this book we have actively started what we believe will be the turning point in the widespread commercial acceptance and ultimate popularity of the science. This means taking the science to the people. In many respects biorhythm is not something that can easily be appreciated without having a visual representation of what it can actually do and how it all works. We became aware of this problem a few years ago when we were involved in trying to attract the interest of many different types of people and organisations – we did not really enjoy much success because the subject was just too involved to get across clearly.

What we have now developed is a computer system that can provide a fast and accurate graphic and text-based guide to biorhythm for anybody who wishes to have a printed report produced for them. Also on the same system we have a compatibility programme which will compare biorhythm compatibility between two people. The service that we have developed is now being operated by a number of retail shops in the UK enabling the general public to have access to a fast, accurate and fashionable biorhythm service that will hopefully generate more interest.

The design considerations that went into this service were very important as it was vital for biorhythm to be presented in a simple and clear way so that the unenlightened would be able easily to recognise the advantages and personal nature of the subject. We have found that this approach has made a vast difference in the attitude of people towards biorhythm. One very popular aspect of the package was the fact that, apart from just showing the biorhythm curves and their calendar, it also has the ability to link a phase table with a daily text summary explaining all your particular conditions for the day in question. This is something that the users of our service have found to be a great help, especially when new to the subject. People getting involved with the science for the first time find that reading the curves can be quite tricky. However, being able to look at the phase table for the day in question and see one's conditions along with an explanation has proved both simple and effective, and when combined with the graphical display, an excellent overall picture is achieved.

With the compatibility service we again felt that the package should be personalised and contain a graphical and text-based view of compatibility, as well as making the subject very clear and easy to follow. The compatibility service also looks at the overall effect of biorhythm compatibility between two people. This is achieved by analysing the ratings that are achieved in each of the three categories and then finding the average between them.

As compatibility is discussed in more detail further on in this book I will only mention a couple of points that are relevant to the examples that you will see on the next few pages. A common mistake among many biorhythm researchers and authors is to assume that, for all three cycles, the highest possible shared day rating is the best. If you examine the Partners Report you can see that the ideal shared day ratings vary with each of the cycles and this point is a very important and often overlooked one. The format of the report is to compare the relevant cycle positions for each partner against the other. This will assist the users to see where their partner will biorhythmically be placed in relation to each of their cycles. Once this has been achieved it is very easy for that person to see what position their partner will be in when they are at a particular stage in each of their cycles. The relative positions between the couple's three biorhythm cycles will always remain constant, i.e. if there was a four-day difference between the start of each partner's physical cycle then it would remain like this on a permanent basis.

Examples of the computerised services that are being produced by The World Biorhythm Club can be seen on the next three pages.

BIORHYTHM REPORT FOR - **Peter Gardner**
DATE OF BIRTH - **Monday 26th February 1962**

Biorhythm Curves for April 1991

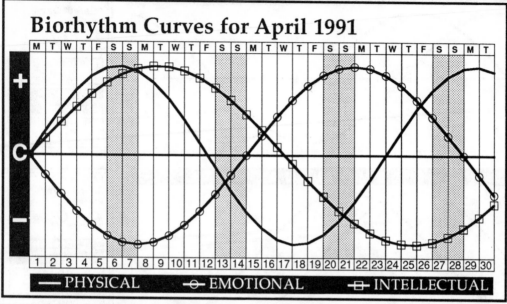

—— PHYSICAL   –o– EMOTIONAL   –⊟– INTELLECTUAL

Biorhythm Phase Table for April 1991

Phase No.	From	To	CONDITION			Outlook
			P	E	I	
1	1st	1st	C	C	C	Sorry Peter but this is the dreaded Triple Critical. This is a day to avoid everything and probably everbody! Take care and don't panic.
2	2nd	11th	+	-	+	Physical energy coupled with mental sharpness is useful in all sorts of activities. Go out and do something fast and furious to avoid feeling down.
3	12th	12th	C	-	+	The accident prone genius! Try and do something mentally demanding. A good day to Physically relax and sort out your finances and budgets.
4	13th	14th	-	-	+	This is a good phase for jobs that require good concentration and little else. Use this time for new subjects or difficult decisions.
5	15th	15th	-	C	-	This is an awkward day, your Critical will make you more touchy than usual, this is a day to do things intelligently and without too much effort.
6	16th	16th	-	+	+	This is a phase for relaxed thinking and creation, you may well be feeling a bit tired. This should be a phase of mental pursuits and activities.
7	17th	17th	-	+	C	Use your positive mood to overcome your lack of energy, this is a day to enjoy life and avoid stressful decision making. Try to have some fun.
8	18th	23rd	-	+	-	Your Emotional high may leave you feeling creative and full of ideas, however save them until your Intellectual cycle goes positive.
9	24th	24th	C	+	-	Creative energy with clumsy tendencies! Although you could be full of ideas, you are open to silly mistakes.. Be creative and careful!
10	25th	28th	+	+	-	A great creative phase with Physical energy and Emotional zest, because you are Intellectually low you can really explore your more wacky ideas.
11	29th	29th	+	C	-	Although you may not feel very sociable today and likely to get upset quickly, your Physical strength should be used to get things done.
12	30th	30th	+	-	-	A good time for Physical tasks that require little thought or planning. Use this phase for more mundane chores. Avoid depressing situations.

Biorhythm Report Example

PETER GARDNER (26-2-1962) & KATE LAWSON (22-4-1967)

PHYSICAL

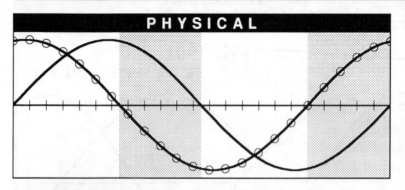

PHYSICAL
Shared Days
Percentage

57%

| EXCELLENT
BIORHYTHMIC
COMPATIBILITY |
| **GOOD**
BIORHYTHMIC
COMPATIBILITY |
| LIMITED
BIORHYTHMIC
COMPATIBILITY |

EMOTIONAL

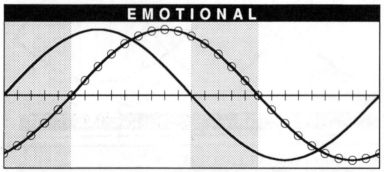

EMOTIONAL
Shared Days
Percentage

64%

| **EXCELLENT**
BIORHYTHMIC
COMPATIBILITY |
| GOOD
BIORHYTHMIC
COMPATIBILITY |
| LIMITED
BIORHYTHMIC
COMPATIBILITY |

INTELLECTUAL

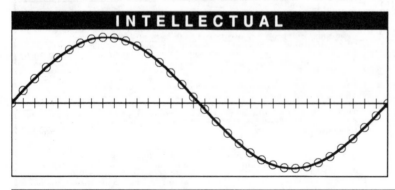

INTELLECTUAL
Shared Days
Percentage

100%

| EXCELLENT
BIORHYTHMIC
COMPATIBILITY |
| **GOOD**
BIORHYTHMIC
COMPATIBILITY |
| LIMITED
BIORHYTHMIC
COMPATIBILITY |

—— PETER'S BIORHYTHM WAVES   ⦵ KATE'S BIORHYTHM WAVES

▭ SHARED DAYS   ▦ NON-SHARED DAYS

Partners Report Example page 1

To calculate a Biorhythm Compatibility you need two people and their respective dates of birth. By comparing their birthdates Biorhythmically, a compatibility picture can be formed. The Graphs on the page show the respective waves and how many days in each one the partners share the same Biorhythm Condition. A 65% Physical Rating for example indicates that in every 23 days - the Physical Cycle length, the partners in question will have the same condition for 15 (65%) of them. High percentages in all three waves does not necessarily mean an overall high level of Compatibility.

The higher the Physical Percentage the better, if a couple have different Physical Conditions for the majority of the time they will find most of the time one partner full of zest and energy in their positive phase and the other in a sleepier negative phase. The ideal Emotional Percentage is 50%, the spread of conditions being 7 days both positive, 7 days both negative and 14 different. Times for fun, understanding and helping one another. High percentage ratings mean the couple will share negative phases for up to 2 weeks at a time. The ideal Intellectual Percentage is around 75%, it is good to have differences here and there to ensure a bit of mental spice! The Intellectual Rhythm controls how organised we are, therefore very high percentages can find both partners overlooking routine chores.

You and Kate are classified as having 'Good' Physical Compatibility. When considering personal relationships Physical Compatibility is obviously a distinct advantage. The Physical Cycle affects how much 'get up and go' we have and if both partners are sharing the same condition for the majority of time they will share similar energy levels. 57% is a good level of Compatibility but remember this percentage also represents the likelihood of Kate sharing the same condition as you. Awareness of your Compatibility is the best way to counteract any problems that may arise from different Physical conditions.

This level of Emotional Compatibility is certainly the most balanced, having a good spread of shared positives, shared negatives and different conditions is the ideal compromise. The Emotional Cycle controls the level of communication and understanding in a relationship and how tolerant the partners are to one another. Excellent Emotional Compatibilty helps the partners avoid silly arguements and problems of non-communication. A point to remember is that for every shared positive there is a shared neagative and in your case this is two periods of 9 days each, in the shared negative phase it will help if you are both aware of your situation.

Intellectual Compatibility is both the most difficult to see the effect of and the least likely to cause a problem in a relationship. The majority of relationships are far more based on Physical attraction and Emotional understanding, and therefore as a Compatibility consideration the Intellectual Cycle is less important. If your relationship is based on a high level of Intellectual interaction then this 'Good' Intellectual Compatibility should find your potential for joint projects well matched. However you do not have enough days where your condition differs from Kate and this could lead to debates going a bit stale.

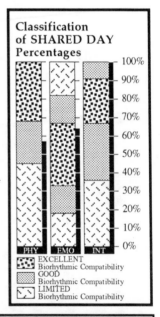

Classification of SHARED DAY Percentages

100%
90%
80%
70%
60%
50%
40%
30%
20%
10%
0%

PHY   EMO   INT

EXCELLENT
Biorhythmic Compatibility
GOOD
Biorhythmic Compatibility
LIMITED
Biorhythmic Compatibility

OVERALL BIORHYTHMIC COMPATIBILITY

	PHYSICAL	EMOTIONAL	INTELLECTUAL
Shared Days	13 OUT OF 23	18 OUT OF 28	33 OUT OF 33
Shared Day Percentage	57%	64%	100%
OPTIMUM Number of SHARED Days	23	14	25
Number of Days from Optimum	10	4	8
COMPATIBILITY Percentage	57%	71%	68%

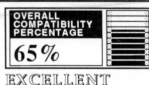

OVERALL COMPATIBILITY PERCENTAGE

65%

EXCELLENT
Overall Biorhythmic
Compatibility

To get the best out of biorhythm, whether as a casual or more serious user, you should investigate some of the many different applications to which the science can interestingly be put. If you like using biorhythm to study subjects that involve people you are interested in, then there is a whole new area of investigation open to you. For example, one of my colleagues is an avid boxing fan and since I introduced him to biorhythm he now religiously checks the biorhythm positions of the boxers involved in a fight that he is going to watch. He finds this a fascinating way of getting far deeper into the analysis of the contest and he is sure of the effects that the science is able to have on the competitors. Not all the situations have been found to correspond to the biorhythm graph for the fighters but far more often than not the result can be directly correlated to the biorhythm conditions at the time. So if you are a boxing manager and you are reading this book, maybe it's time you tried a little applied biorhythm on your fighters.

A new application of biorhythm which is just being introduced into the UK is as an aid to slimming. The basic idea for this concept is to time a slimming programme to correspond to the biorhythm conditions that affect you at the time. It has been found that one's so called 'will power' can be linked to the emotional and intellectual cycle positions. Being in a positive and intelligent frame of mind will obviously make the mental task of coping with a slimming programme that much easier, so this should be taken into account before and during a diet. With this concept it should be far easier for a person on a diet to realise that when the going starts to get tough it will hopefully not be too long before one of these two cycles moves into a positive phase to help retain mental composure. A common observation is that when somebody on a diet gives up or even has a one-day binge their will to continue is often lost. An understanding of your biorhythm condition can help ensure that these little slips are only temporary ones.

The most common application of biorhythm, however, is the

personal one where an individual will be using the science to improve his or her life and to plan ahead. Biorhythm used in this way will enable the individual to realise and, hopefully, achieve a very close harmony with their body. The advantages and uses for the science can obviously be harnessed into the bargain; it all depends on how much you want to get out of biorhythm.

There is no guarantee that biorhythm will change the way you view your life and in many ways it should not really do so, but if the correct approach is followed then there is a very strong likelihood that the science will offer you real benefits in many different circumstances. Biorhythm is just one of many different forms of insight that exist, some better than others, some based on fact and some based on myth. Biorhythm, it could be said, has a lot going for it and certainly has enough of a proven background seriously to be considered as a subject that is at least able to stand up to most of the claims that it makes. As far as understanding why the science works in the way that it does, this will not be resolved for some time yet as the research and medical knowledge required to establish what exactly it is that drives our internal clocks with such accuracy is something with which the more established sciences are still coming to terms.

BIORHYTHM TOMORROW

What the future holds for biorhythm is still a little unclear. It may well be that the science will never really make it right to the top of the popularity tree, or it may explode onto the world stage in a flash of glory. The outcome depends very much on the attitude of the people who set the trend for new fashions and new products in the marketplace.

The work that we are carrying out is the first stage towards taking biorhythm out of its 1970s mould and giving the whole subject a real facelift. The development of some very advanced computer software has helped enormously in allowing us to develop biorhythm programmes that would previously have required an extremely powerful and expensive system to run them. The advantage of hi-tech modern-day computer packages is that we can effectively take a subject that has in the past been very much a 'do it yourself' thing and turn it into something that can be run in a matter of minutes! Of course, for the critics who are not prepared to accept the theory a method has to be employed to change their opinions, and the best way of achieving this is with proof. The published research that has been carried out to date, while impressive, is now a number of years old and is, therefore, considered by some to be insufficient evidence. What is needed is new material that can be examined within strict parameters and under official guidance, to give it the chance of being socially accepted. This would open the door to more printed material on the subject and, in essence, start the ball rolling again on a subject that has been far too quiet for far too long.

2

HOW BIORHYTHM WORKS

So what is the theory behind this science and how is it possible to access and practically employ this window into the future? Biorhythm is made up of three distinct cycles, all of which follow the pattern of a sinusoidal curve, differing only in the amount of time that they each take to complete their full cycle length.

Each cycle represents one particular function only. The first category is the physical cycle. It is the shortest of the three at 23 days long, and influences our health and vitality. The emotional cycle follows next, having a span of 28 days, which is a very interesting length when applying biorhythm in our daily lives, because it is divisible by the seven days of the week. The emotional cycle plays a leading role in determining our moods and creativity as well as our enthusiasm towards certain activities or challenges that we may encounter. The final and longest cycle is the intellectual with a duration of 33 days. The intellectual cycle is responsible for our ability to absorb, and then act upon information, with large differences in this particular ability being clearly shown in most individuals during the different phases of the cycle. (*See page 30.*)

Each of the three cycles commences from a person's exact moment of birth, and then continues in a never-ending and totally consistent pattern for the rest of one's life. The cycles soon move out of sync a few days after birth and will not return to their original start point until the common denominator between them is reached. After exactly 21,252 days the position of each of the cycles will be indentical to the point where they began. Between these dates all of the possible biorhythm combinations will be experienced. All the cycles contain three particular phases which are common to them all, namely the positive, negative and

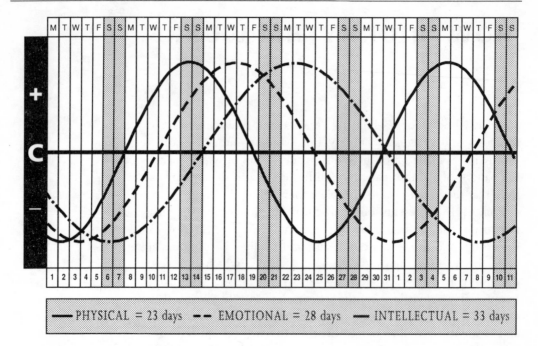

— PHYSICAL = 23 days - - EMOTIONAL = 28 days — INTELLECTUAL = 33 days

The Biorhythm Cycles

critical phases. The positive phase, which takes approximately half the total cycle length (in all cases), will bring with it a period dominated by the favourable aspects that are characteristic to that particular cycle or rhythm.

To explain in more detail, if you were in a period where your emotional cycle was enjoying a good positive position then it would be likely that you would find yourself in good spirits and feeling very optimistic and confident about the future. The negative phase, identical to the positive in length, has virtually the opposite effect, for example, periods of negative cycle influences will leave an individual feeling tired (physical negative) or depressed (emotional negative). The most interesting phase is that of the critical day. It is referred to as a day because this phase is exactly 24 hours long. The critical day is the period when a cycle is changing from positive to negative or vice versa, which in turn induces within the body a period of imbalance for the individual concerned. The effects are magnified if two and especially all three of the cycles are critical at the same time. The critical day has been linked to times when we are far more likely to suffer self-caused accidents as a result of this imbalance in our behavioural patterns. The characteristics of each phase for each cycle are covered in detail further on in this chapter.

The overall effects of biorhythm are to be found when one studies all three biorhythm categories together. While each one of the categories can and will have influence over an individual, it is only when all three are carefully considered as a group that the actual effect upon the individual concerned can be calculated with any sort of accuracy. It is important to recognise that the strong aspects of one or two of the cycles at a given time can help to compensate for a weak position in one of the other cycles.

A little basic maths knowledge will tell you that if you have three different categories (physical, emotional and intellectual) and three possible conditions (positive, negative and critical) then, in basic terms, there are really only 27 different combinations that can exist between the three categories on any one day, although once you have entered a particular 24-hour period, your condition will remain the same for that day. It is the study of the interactions of these three ever-changing cycles that will reveal new depths of potential and awareness in us all. The time that we spend in each of the 27 different combinations will vary, but no one set of conditions will last for more than eleven days.

Understanding the effects of these interactions comes with experience, and this is best gained by relating the subtle changes which we are able to detect within ourselves during our daily routines, and comparing them to our changing biorhythm condition. If biorhythm does work then it would be logical to assume that some variation in our normal performance or behaviour would show up on our biorhythm graph. While this statement is usually borne out it should be noted that external influences have a part in producing results that contradict what biorhythm would indicate. For example, if you were planning to take part in a ten-mile run in the morning and your biorhythm position was in a favourable physical condition, but you over-indulged yourself in whatever form the previous night, then it would be safe to assume that your performance would suffer as a result of the admittedly enjoyable but totally reckless behaviour the evening before.

As biorhythm is a science which identifies changes of a subtle nature which can go unnoticed in the course of our daily lives, it is normally only in those challenging situations that the significant influence of biorhythm can be readily observed.

THE PHYSICAL CYCLE

The physical cycle has a duration of 23 days and is primarily concerned with the effectiveness of our bodily functions. Our ability to perform those tasks that require a degree of strength, stamina and coordination will almost certainly be influenced by the prevailing physical cycle.

The Positive Phase

Examination of the positive phase shows that it reaches a peak roughly six days after the start of the cycle. This peak is significant in the analysis of the positive phase. The build-up to the peak is the most advantageous period of the physical cycle, as once the peak has been passed the cycle is then on its way down, meaning that whilst still being positive its power and strength are diminishing slightly with every day. If you compare this observation with an athlete in training you would notice that training programmes are geared to peak exactly at the moment of ultimate competition. Many competitors have trained too hard

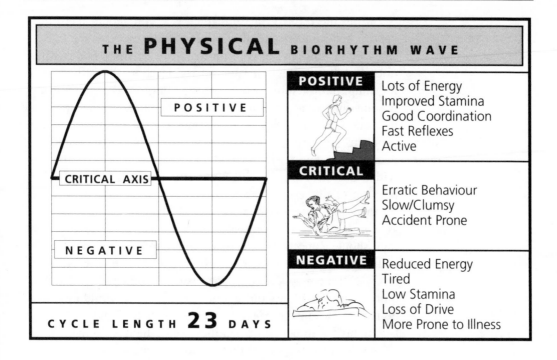

THE **PHYSICAL** BIORHYTHM WAVE	
POSITIVE	Lots of Energy Improved Stamina Good Coordination Fast Reflexes Active
CRITICAL	Erratic Behaviour Slow/Clumsy Accident Prone
NEGATIVE	Reduced Energy Tired Low Stamina Loss of Drive More Prone to Illness

CYCLE LENGTH **23** DAYS

and peaked too early for competitions and have found that they were at their best a few days too early. Likewise with the biorhythm cycle: it is simply not possible to be at your best indefinitely – there has to be a building-up and an easing down period.

Generally, however, the analysis of the positive phase does not take into account whether the cycle is in an upswing or a downward swing. This generalisation is really quite sufficient for most applications of the physical cycle as there is no substantial difference between any one day within the confines of the positive phase, or of the negative phase. If, however, you are using biorhythm as a training aid and you want ultimate accuracy in the timing of your programme, then the more detailed analysis showing the exact day-to-day conditions is a worthwhile exercise.

During the positive phase of the cycle you should feel full of energy and vitality, and this pleasant state of existence will be reflected in a number of your normal daily activities. For example, nobody likes turning up late and red-faced at the office in the morning, but for some people getting out of bed in the mornings is something that can cause serious difficulties. People often call it laziness but the fact is that some people do have genuine problems in raising themselves from sleep. Such people can benefit from knowledge of their physical cycle because the ease with which they are able to get out of bed will be reflected by the position of this cycle. During the positive phase it will be easier for them to 'come round' and shake off the effects of a deep sleep as their bodies, once conscious, have higher energy levels. What they should concentrate on is making sure that they are getting sufficient sleep during their negative phase so as to rebuild energy reserves. If these people enjoy socialising at night and tend to have quite a few late nights throughout the month it would definitely be to their advantage to try to arrange their evenings so that the late nights fall in periods when they are in the positive part of the cycle so as to make use of their accumulated energy.

Another of the observed advantages of the positive phase of the cycle is the increased efficiency of the body's reflexes and coordination. Numerous tests and studies have been carried out to determine how an individual's hand and eye coordination varies over time. During the positive phase many operations such as typing or reacting on the brakes in potentially dangerous driving situations have been measured. In most instances the positive phase shows a speed increase of around ten per cent over the negative and especially critical aspects of the cycle.

In the sports world many activities require players with speed, timing, fast reflexes and good coordination. The positive aspect of the physical cycle can further enhance and sharpen all of these assets and so pre-planning and scheduling the preparation and training towards an event can help turn a good performance into a brilliant one.

In matters of health and fitness the positive effects of this cycle can also have very useful advantages. Most of the research work that was conducted by Wilhelm Fleiss centred on the fluctuations of the body's ability to resist disease and infection. This type of research found that the body had definite and consistent cycles that would alter the effectiveness of our basic immune system. The human body as a rule will be far more resistant to infections and disease during the positive period of the physical cycle. The same will also apply to the strength and durability of muscles ligaments and tendons, so reducing the likelihood of getting pulls and strains during exercise and sporting activity.

The Negative Phase

The negative phase begins on day thirteen of the physical cycle and during this period the body will be operating below its best. Energy levels are low and it is a time that should be spent, if possible, concentrating on aspects other than physical activity. This is not to say that you can't get involved in any form of sport or healthy exercise, but it is important to remember that you will be slightly off-peak and need to take care not to overexert yourself. The people who would really feel the difference in their performance would be top class athletes and sportsmen whose competitive margins are often measured in tenths or even hundredths of a second. It is people such as this who can really benefit from awareness of their physical cycle position.

For the individual who is interested in getting the best out of their performance, whatever activity it is that they find themselves in, there is always an opportunity for applied biorhythm. Although with most sports it is not possible to choose the time and date to compete, the dates are normally known in advance which will enable you to analyse your biorhythm position beforehand and adjust your strategy for the event accordingly. If you find that a negative physical condition is going to prevail on the day in question then there are a number of things that can be done. First, it would useful to check the position of your other cycles, the reason being to establish whether there are any alternative strengths indicated by them which you may call upon for your game or event. For example, a strong intellectual and emotional condition would almost certainly help to reduce the effect of the negative physical cycle. This is to say that by knowing the effects of the physical negative, you will be able to use your intellectual positive to pre-plan your tactics so that you can turn the problem to your best advantage. For example, when playing badminton in this condition, one should try to concentrate one's intellectual efforts into outwitting the opponent by placing shots in a position calculated to be unreachable, as opposed to a smash it and run approach, which would tire one out by the second game. If successful, it would be a classic example of 'brains beating brawn'. A high emotional position can give one added confidence. Another option that is open is pre-event practice or training which may enable one to resolve any particular faults within one's game which may cause trouble at a particular point in one's cycle. It is quite likely that during this period one may actually be in a strong physical condition, which would obviously be a good time for extra training. The third and probably slightly unsporting option would be to cancel or reschedule a game if it is important, for a more biorhythmically suitable time.

The Critical Day

The physical critical day falls both at the start and on day twelve of the physical cycle. The influence of the critical day on our performance and behaviour has to be seen, or rather felt, to be believed. Any of the biorhythm cynics would probably laugh if you told them that on these critical days, an individual is far more likely to suffer a self-caused accident. This is based on the information gained by the many studies that we, and other research groups, have carried out. In the physical cycle the critical day has a very strong effect on the coordination and general togetherness of movement.

On a critical day you will almost certainly find that your reaction speed and physical coordination will be well below par and, unfortunately for a lot of people, this results all too frequently in an accident. Accidents could often be avoided if reaction time and physical coordination were faster and more controlled. The effective communication between the brain and the body is simply not as quick as normal on the critical day, and this causes problems if we are not aware of our biorhythm condition in advance and, therefore, take it as read that all our body movements are not working as they normally would.

In the many cases that we have been asked by family, friends and others for a personalised biorhythm chart, the request usually results from an awareness that one's performance does indeed vary from one day to another for no apparent reason. This is to some extent the beginning of biorhythm awareness, the acceptance of changing internal potential that is not affected by outside sources.

The outside world obviously plays a major part in how we feel and perform, but in terms of effect biorhythm is a constant background function that can be monitored by anyone. Interest in the biorhythm plot usually begins on a fun basis. Everyone has an interest in information about themselves, but this interest is deepened when it is found that a correlation exists between themselves and their biorhythm chart. In the same way that people react differently to the same events around them, the effects of biorhythm from person to person alter. Some people are truly inspired by a moving piece of classical music whereas others are left cold, and biorhythm conditions act upon people in the same way. Creative people tend to more interested in their inspirational emotional rhythm rather than their prevailing physical condition.

In the many cases we have come across, accidents and events out of the ordinary prompt people to consult biorhythm for a possible explanation, and in the majority of cases there is a critical condition to accompany these events. This obviously does not even class as a reactive use of biorhythm, and the irony is that the information is available to anyone. The effective and pro-active use of biorhythm is to know your conditions in advance and take the necessary precautions.

Most people who check their biorhythm position in the morning will usually forget all about their cycle positions until something out of the ordinary reminds them that they may be under the influence of a particular phase. To be fully aware of your strengths and weaknesses during the day requires an almost religious application to biorhythm, so the best way to avoid the unnecessary is to try to reflect on your strengths and weaknesses *before* you tackle something that requires a little more care or thought than most normal tasks. This strategy has been found to work extremely well because the effects of biorhythm are usually felt most strongly when we are challenged physically, emotionally or intellectually in circumstances that are more than just routine.

In the field of medicine a number of Swiss clinics have used biorhythm as an aid to knowing the precise condition of their patients. They have taken the view that this form of study is both accessible and has a large potential for helping them plan treatments and operations. Very little research work is available in this field but some of the studies that have been done indicate that there is a strong case for scheduling routine surgery in accordance with the physical biorhythm of the patient concerned. If, for example, the operation is carried out at the beginning of the third day in the physical rhythm, then the patient will have over a week of optimum strength and recovery powers. This is not suggesting that biorhythm can be used to save lives directly, but it can play its role in giving the patient the best possible chance of survival. Another point to consider is the financial implication of implementing such a scheme. Biorhythm is not expensive, nor does it require experienced technicians. It can be used cheaply and conveniently and, most importantly, it does not stand in the way of medical knowledge. Biorhythm simply offers the doctors concerned more information to make a better decision.

However, it is important to remember that most of the effects of this particular cycle are relatively harmless in most forms of exercise and healthy activity especially in people who already enjoy a good level of fitness. What should be avoided, however, is over-exertion. Anybody, however fit, can push themselves too far, which in any biorhythm position can be potentially dangerous, but during a physical critical it could result in a painful and even fatal outcome. The body is not able to cope well with very strenuous activity during this type of day and the chances are that overexertion will lead to some form of injury; something that can be avoided if you take heed of the biorhythm warning.

The 28-day emotional cycle will have an influence on the way we feel about ourselves and the people and situations around us. This cycle will also play a large part in our ability to be creative and generate ideas as well determining whether we will be confident or secure about the many situations that present themselves to us on a daily basis.

THE EMOTIONAL CYCLE

Having an optimistic, yet at the same time realistic outlook on life can mean the difference between success and failure. For some of us the actual effects of the emotional cycle are so pronounced they can easily be felt and judged without even referring to a biorhythm chart. The positive phase of the cycle will often enable an individual to look towards the future with intense optimism even in the bleakest moments. This interesting effect of the cycle will often make people push that little bit harder to achieve the goals that they secretly know are achievable with a lot of hard work and determination.

From the diagram on page 40 you can see that the peak of the

The Positive Phase

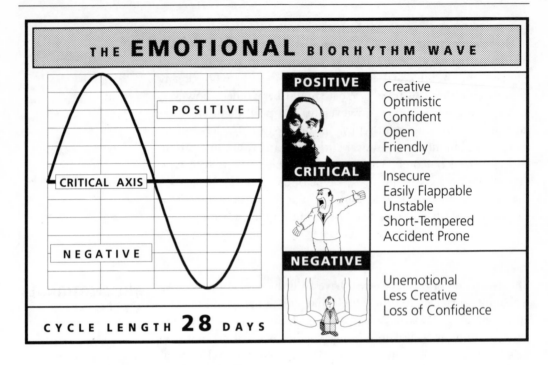

cycle is reached after seven days and the positive phase finishes its span after fourteen days. During this phase it is important to not get over-confident in your abilities as this can obviously lead to problematic and even dangerous situations. It is important always to take into account the factors that prevail in your other two cycles when considering any decisions that are taken as a result of any emotional high that you may be experiencing. An example of this can be related to an incident that took place just prior to a large Battle of Britain air show in England during the autumn of 1988.

On the day before the show an RAF Phantom jet was carrying out a training run with two crew members aboard. They were attempting a 'loop the loop' manoeuvre in preparation for the

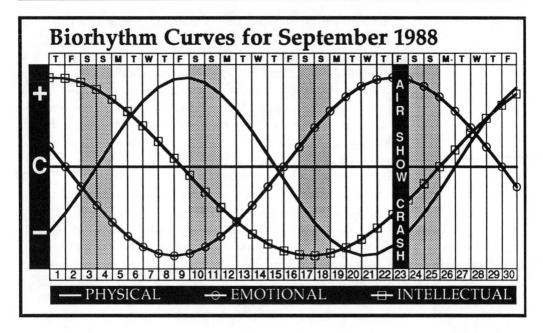

Biorhythm Curves for September 1988

AIR SHOW CRASH

— PHYSICAL   —⊙— EMOTIONAL   —⊟— INTELLECTUAL

RAF Crash

display. Halfway through the routine the aircraft plunged into the ground exploding into flames. Tragically both the pilot and navigator were killed in the accident.

A subsequent inquest failed to find a cause for the accident. No problems were found with the aircraft and the weather conditions were ideal. Witnesses said that the jet simply failed to pull out of the dive that made up the last part of the loop. The official verdict on the accident was that of accidental death. As you can see from the diagram, on the day in question the pilot was under the influence of an emotional high that was virtually at the peak of the cycle but this was combined with negative conditions in both the physical and intellectual cycles. The accident could have been caused by a case of over-confidence that was not backed up with the ability to actually pull off the manoeuvre which they believed to be possible.

Another, less sobering, effect of the emotional positive is that individuals are far more likely to be creative and generate a lot of new ideas during this phase. The reason for this is quite simple in concept: during periods of optimism and confidence the mind does not seem to be bogged down with worry or problems, leaving it open to thought without too many obstacles. The generation of new ideas and plans is something that can obviously reap large rewards, but during this period it is possible to get too optimistic about something, so it is important always to review your decision during a period when you are not on quite such a high. If you are both emotionally and intellectually positive during these great brainstorming sessions then it is likely that some of the ideas that you come up with are nothing less than brilliant.

The Negative Phase

The negative phase of the emotional cycle can be a time when you show some of the less pleasant aspects of your character. This period will often find you in low spirits, especially if things aren't going that well for you at the time. With biorhythm the cycle phases can intensify or even blow out of proportion the particular events that are taking place around you. For example, if you have just had an argument with your loved one and you are also in the depths of an emotional negative, a feeling quite similar to that of the world caving in on you is not uncommon. A strong sense of injustice will usually prevail as you will probably be unable to find fault with your behaviour.

During this period your sympathies will almost certainly lie only with yourself. This is why, for most of us who are guilty of having to apologise to people for our out-of-character behaviour, it is important to be aware of these times when our patience and rationality are not what they might be. We are not saying that awareness of this particular phase will make us into saints but it can definitely help us to be more tolerant and sympathetic. Most of us regret having upset someone at some time, and even though as we get older we tend to mellow, biorhythm offers a real opportunity to improve this trait that lies in our innermost personalities.

Of all the phases that exist within biorhythm, the negative emotional is the one that can really put us down in the dumps. One should not forget though that this phase can, like all the others, be influenced and affected by external factors. Even the serious argument with your loved one would probably pale into insignificance if you suddenly won a million in a prize draw. Back in reality, however, even if you were in a positive phase in the other two cycles and thus ideally suited to the task in hand, your inclination may simply not be there to carry out that activity. We have found that during these difficult and depressing periods there is a way to beat the gloom. It is a case of applying yourself to a different task that is well suited to you and can be done well with a low-key emotional position. The purpose for this is twofold, in that in certain situations your low emotional outlook would not actually be a hindrance to getting the job done. Often the best tasks to tackle are ones that can bring a sense of achievement when completed. Sitting around and not getting anything done does not really aid your recovery from depression.

Awareness of your emotional negative can also improve your chances in many competitive activities especially if your are someone who is driven by emotions. Determination is a factor that will have a large bearing on the amount of effort that you may put into a performance, and it would be very wasteful to give up on yourself before an event. Pre-knowledge of your complete biorhythm picture could dramatically alter your feelings and ultimately your hunger for success. With many professional sportsmen, a coach or trainer is there to motivate and 'pump up' the competitor, whereas your motivating factor will be the potential strong points in your other cycles. For example, if you are going into competition with a low-key emotional cycle but your physical and intellectual cycles are very positive, then the reality of what you could actually achieve as opposed to your lack of will should help to push you to a better result than you previously thought possible.

The Critical Day

The emotional critical day occurs exactly every fourteen days which means that it shouldn't be too difficult to remember what day of the week it is that you will suffer this condition. If you are critical in this cycle on a Monday for example, then you will always have a critical every other Monday for the rest of your life – a depressing but reliable thought!

The effects of this day are considered to be one of the most dangerous of all the biorhythm conditions that can be encountered. This is because decision making and matters of judgement will tend to be badly distorted, and often decisions taken on this type of day are of a spur of the moment nature that can lead to dangerous or unpleasant outcomes. During these days if an individual is put under pressure they may often react totally out of character, with what can only be described as extremely rash behaviour.

The unpredictability of actions on these days has been shown, in research into activities requiring careful and precise operation, to leave us open to accidents. We all have reservations about certain things that we are asked to do at some time or other in our lives, especially if we feel it could be dangerous, and when we don't feel too sure about the outcome we would normally decline the offer. However, on the seven per cent of days which are emotionally critical for us the answer might not always be 'no', which could lead to unfortunate outcomes. In relationships, an emotional critical in either one of a couple's cycles can often lead to tears, as an outburst or unkind comment will probably spark a row, especially if the other partner's biorhythm condition is not favourably placed to the handling of such a situation. It seems that on these days anybody can suddenly become a target for cruel or cutting comments without any real provocation. To totally blame this type of irrational behaviour on biorhythm is not really acceptable but there is no doubt that the emotional critical will certainly light the short fuse that ignites the bomb.

It should be noted that these side-effects of the critical condition will affect people with differing intensity. There is no doubt that some people do not show some of the bad-tempered traits that most of us have, as often they will keep them buried inside while still remaining calm and composed on the outside. A colleague who is a graphic designer is affected strongly by this critical, but in him it doesn't usually bring out any aggressive or irrational outbursts as he is generally a very relaxed character. What it does affect, however, is his creative ability. Artists tend to be driven by emotion when they are creating and he is certainly no exception. His best and most creative work will usually be in the positive phase of the emotional cycle. During the negative phase he will not be quite as original but is still able to work, especially if he operates during the evening, for which he has a distinct preference. On the critical days, however, he says that he suffers from a total blank state of mind when trying to create new visual concepts and will only get edgy and withdrawn if pressure is put on him to finish a job during this phase. His solution to this potentially wasted day is to concentrate on other aspects of his job that don't rely quite so much on creative thinking, such as checking for errors on a job that is in progress or simply concentrating on other matters that need to be attended to such as his administration and accounts.

The 33-day intellectual cycle determines how effective our brain is at assessing and planning our lives. It is primarily concerned with our capacity for thought and the rationalisation of those thoughts.

THE INTELLECTUAL CYCLE

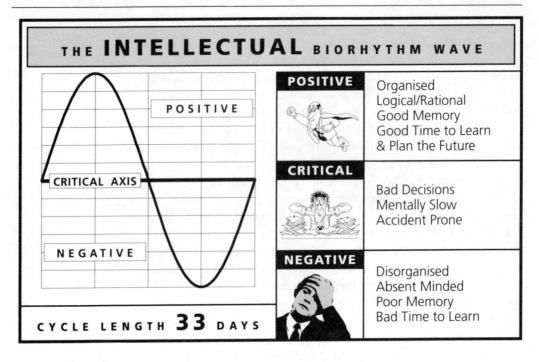

The Positive Phase

Finding oneself in the positive phase of this cycle will almost certainly hold many advantages for all of us. To be 'on top' and fully in control of affairs requires planning and a certain amount of regime. It's all too easy to let things slip and become disorganised with items such as bills, appointments, and the busy schedule of work at the office to name a few. The intellectual positive phase is definitely the best time to capitalise on getting these types of situation back under control. It is during this period, especially approaching the peak of the cycle (which you can see from the diagram is eight days after the start), that your ability to use the powers of your brain is at its best.

Everybody, young or old, is constantly faced with problems that test mental aptitude, and it is a fact that we deal with these problems with differing efficiency on different days. Much of the research carried out by Alfred Teltscher was centred around the learning curves and performance of his students over a prolonged period of time. His results were conclusive and in accordance with more recent work which also showed that this cycle can show very beneficial effects in young children whose brains are absorbing and learning new information at a staggering rate when compared to a fully matured adult.

Intensive teaching during the positive phase has often produced astounding results. More and more parents have applied this technique to their children and recently in England a father who had made use of this biorhythm guidance achieved such remarkable results that he was featured in the national press with his son who, despite being only four years of age, could already read, write, and undertake basic arithmetic calculations. In this case he simply applied the positive phase calculation to his son and carried out extra tuition during this period. During these periods his son's brain was not only more able to take on new information, he was also more prepared to do so, positively thriving on the opportunity to exercise this much under-used organ!

In many cases the heightened awareness that accompanies this condition can play a real part in avoiding accidents and mistakes that one would normally walk straight into. Attention to detail is dealt with almost subconsciously during this phase and many things that would normally go unnoticed are identified with beneficial results. It needn't always be a dramatic situation that is avoided. For example, your car may be losing water through a split radiator hose and you actually notice that the temperature gauge is rising above normal and are able to do something about the situation before any serious damage has occurred. If you consider this to be an obvious example then just try and remember just how much attention you normally pay to the less used instruments in your car.

The intellectual positive phase could prove to be a valuable time if you actually bother to use it to its potential even if you don't suffer from being unorganised or put under pressure. Most of us have had dreams of being successful and making money but more often than not our time is spent hoping that we will get a lucky break, whereas in real life you have to do something that can bring opportunity in your direction. The best way to apply the power of the intellectual cycle is to set aside a time during the positive phase to see if you can find any opportunities that may set you on your way to success.

There are so many ways that you can utilise this aspect of the intellectual cycle and really the best way to find out how successfully to apply it to yourself is to try a number of different situations and see what benefits you get; it is almost a case of trial and error.

The Negative Phase

During this phase matters that require more than ordinary thought or mental ability can cause problems. The ability to analyse and absorb information is nowhere near as efficient as in the positive stage of the cycle. It is at such times that the old saying 'in one ear and out of the other' comes to mind. One's mind will be easily attracted by anything that takes it away from what will often seem tedious and difficult, and even looking at the windows being cleaned outside the office can seem far more interesting than sorting out the problems that are waiting for you on the desk. We all suffer from periods of thinking that perhaps we are not suited to the office life and maybe an outdoor existence in the fresh air would be far more enjoyable, so before applying for that gamekeeper's job you saw advertised, you should take a peek at your biorhythms.

There really is not too much that can be done about the dulling of mental performance during these periods but in most cases the effects are not really that powerful until the cycle is at the bottom of its span, around days 24 to 27 of the 33-day cycle. If you are able to concentrate on matters other than those requiring mental agility then you won't have a problem with this period but unfortunately for most of us, the daily routine of our lives does not give us the opportunity to choose when such matters present themselves. If you are aware that you will be encountering this trough during a testing time at work then it is important that you try to plan ahead and give yourself the best possible chance of coming through this period without making too many mistakes. For example, it might not be a bad idea to put in a bit of overtime a few days before the onset of an intellectual negative period so that you can get ahead of yourself with any mentally difficult work, thereby removing the potential problem altogether.

Outside of the office environment there are a number of things that could be concentrated on during this type of phase. If you look at your physical and emotional categories you may find it is a good time for you to concentrate on sport and exercise or spend some time socialising with friends. It is really just a case of scheduling activities that are best suited to your biorhythmic disposition at the time. If this format is applied regularly you will find that you are getting the best out of the time that you have, so much so that it will seem like you have actually got more time than normal.

The Critical Day

Generally speaking the symptoms of this day are a mind that will not focus properly on the tasks in hand, along with a tendency to get confused with issues that normally would not even cause a second thought. Other problems associated with this cycle position are the reduced abilities of our memory; it is all too easy to overlook things during an intellectual critical. In most cases this flaw in your ability to perform certain tasks as efficiently as you would wish shouldn't lead to any serious problems, but of course a lot will depend on what particular activity it is that you are doing at the time. If, for example, you are an aircraft technician, then a lapse in concentration or forgetting to carry out a particular check could possibly lead to disaster. If you find yourself involved in a field that really requires attention to detail and has a safety-conscious element, then it is vital that you are aware of the position of your intellectual critical days and take note to be a little more systematic in your approach.

When considering accident prevention with biorhythm, it is important fully to realise what effect this slightly confused and out of balance intellectual condition could have on your safety in a large number of situations in which you will find yourself. If, for example, you are driving during this day, then it is vital that you follow a careful and strategic method. It is wise to question your judgement, as it is all too common an occurrence to find accidents that happen on this day are due to 'poor judgement' which in other less diplomatic terms means a self-caused accident that was totally avoidable with the right precautions.

In the office situation the person that makes a number of important business decisions every day should take care to act cautiously during the intellectual critical day. Everybody makes bad decisions now and again, but for the big decision-maker these mistakes can be costly. As a significant percentage of decisions will *have* to be taken on this critical day, then the importance of self-awareness of this condition is obvious.

The good news is that the intellectual critical is the type of condition that can be guarded against with a little preparation. All that is required is really to consider the implications of what you are doing, in whatever field of activity, and to look at the likely outcomes from the decisions that you may make. In normal circumstances you would probably make the right decision or do the job right because the overriding factors that influence you in your task are clear to you, but during the critical day it may be necessary almost to consider them out loud or from written notes so that you can review them fully.

You should, by now, have a reasonable understanding of the principles that go to make up the science of biorhythm. The mathematics behind the science are very straightforward in terms of calculation complexity, but they do require complete accuracy in order to get the correct condition information. It is important to remember that because your biorhythm condition is directly linked to the number of days you have lived and as nearly everybody has been alive for a different number of days, respective biorhythm conditions will always appear to be different.

THE MATHEMATICAL PRINCIPLES

The formula for establishing your biorhythm position on any given day is simply a question of establishing the total number of days that you have been alive and then dividing that number by the respective cycle length to find the mathematical remainder. This remainder indicates how far into the particular cycle you are for the day in question.

In the case of a baby born on 1 January, 1991, the calculation to establish the biorhythm position 40 days after birth is as follows:

Physical position: $40 \div 23 = 1$ remainder 17
Emotional position: $40 \div 28 = 1$ remainder 12
Intellectual position: $40 \div 33 = 1$ remainder 7

Therefore when any child is 40 days old their biorhythm positions will be:

Physical	17
Emotional	12
Intellectual	7

As can be seen from the example, the important number in the calculation is the remainder. The integer number in the calculation merely indicates how many complete cycles have been experienced since birth.

The following biorhythm graph shows the first 40 days in a child's life. You will also see that biorhythm is best expressed as a visual object rather than simply dealing with a series of numbers and then trying to work out exactly where they will be placed on an imaginary biorhythm graph. Once a visual appreciation of the biorhythm chart is obtained it is much easier and far more revealing to work with. The obvious advantage of this is that apart from just looking at the one day in question, you can also study at the same time those days leading up to and beyond that day.

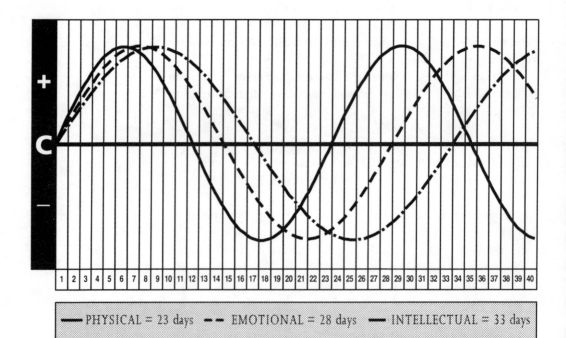

PHYSICAL = 23 days   EMOTIONAL = 28 days   INTELLECTUAL = 33 days

The First Forty Days of Life

Biorhythm is a very accurate science and the calculations required need to be precise. In many cases of intense research the time of birth can be an important factor in determining the exact effect of the critical day. The problem is that the normal biorhythm calculation does not take into account that some people are born just as one day is ending or the next is beginning. In these cases, in order to achieve an accurate biorhythm picture it is necessary to compensate by bringing the date of birth figure forward by one day. Most common biorhythm calculators or methods that have been available to date do not take the time of birth into account. When you are using the biorhythm calculator and plastic transparencies in this book you might like to take your hour of birth into account and, if necessary, shift the scale one day forward or back accordingly. In most cases this level of accuracy is not really required to benefit from the science.

Once the biorhythm cycles have begun their life it is over 58 years before they all meet again, exactly at the start of their respective cycles. This day is a triple critical and is achieved after exactly 21,252 days. This is the lowest common denominator between the 23-, 28- and 33-day cycles, as all the cycle lengths multiplied together will equal this figure. It is, however, possible to have a triple critical day before this period as there are a number of other alternative combinations that exist between the cycles which could cause this fateful event. In absolute terms then, there are 21,252 different cycle conditions that exist between the three categories. This is because although we only use 27 basic permutations, there are thousands of small-detail cycle changes that occur within these overall parameters which don't alter the overall biorhythm picture. For example, if you were in a triple positive one day, the next day all your rhythms would have moved on by one day, but may still leave you in a triple positive situation, being just a little further on in their cycles than on the previous day. It is this type of analysis that accounts for the staggeringly huge number of minor combinations that exist within the science. Very accurate study of biorhythm calls for this amount of detailed examination, the determining of not just which phase each of the cycles are at but whether, for example, they are at their peak or in a downward swing. However, for the purposes of day-to-day biorhythm implementation it is more than sufficient simply to apply the overall phases on their own.

Within this formula lies the critical day which is an intrinsic part of each of the three cycles. The critical day, as we have said, is 24 hours long and a few different opinions exist as to when it starts in relation to the actual position of the cycle. The main and most sound theory is that it actually begins 12 hours before the cycle crosses the mid point line and completes its span 12 hours after crossing this point. There is also a complimentary theory that would seem to hold a certain amount of validity, which is that your first critical period actually starts approximately 12 hours before birth, possibly linked to the breaking of the mother's water. This period and up to 12 hours or so after birth is the most important and critical part of a baby's life. This is why it can be important to know your exact time of birth so that you can effectively fine tune your critical day position.

The frequency at which these critical days occur is easily calculated. Take a 365-day period and count all the criticals that would occur in each cycle, which will bring you to a figure of around 90 critical days in total for the three cycles combined. Most of these would occur as single critical days but there would also be a number of double criticals and possibly a triple critical. Expressed as a percentage, you can see that a total of 90 criticals in a 365-day year equates to approximately 25 per cent or one day in every four.

Many of the research programmes that have been carried out on biorhythm and the critical day have tried to establish whether a higher than expected percentage of self-caused accidents occur on the 25 per cent of days which are termed critical. Most of the results that have been collated on this subject have shown that a higher than normal incidence does occur on these days, often attracting up to 70 per cent of self-caused accidents, which is, statistically speaking, almost triple that which would be expected.

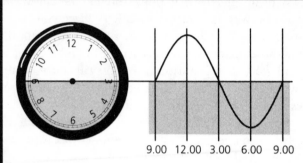

The positive period of each wave occurs in the first half of each full cycle.

The critical axis is crossed every time the condition changes.

The negative period of each wave occurs in the second half of each full cycle.

9.00   12.00   3.00   6.00   9.00

The pattern that each biorhythm wave takes follows the principle of a sine curve. A biorhythm wave behaves like a hand on a clockface; beginning at 9.00 it builds to its high at 12.00, then changes to negative at 3.00, falling to its lowest point at 6.00, and finally finishes back at 9.00 ready to repeat itself. The critical axis is where the clock changes from positive to negative or negative to positive. It is during this period of change that you have an increased likelihood of suffering a self-caused accident. The three waves differ from one another in the amount of time it takes for their 'hands' to complete one full circle of the clock face. In the case of the physical wave this imaginary clock will take 23 days to complete one full revolution.

Anatomy of a Sine Wave

Once you are familiar with the principles of the science and are able to evaluate the particular conditions for a given day, then the interpretation of what those actual conditions mean is the next step to getting the most out of biorhythm. As we have already discussed the three categories on an individual basis, it is useful fully to appreciate the effect of these categories when considered together.

Some of the categories can be influenced by the prevailing conditions in any of the other cycles, and this can either amplify or reduce the effects of one of the cycles concerned. Consequently the analysis of this situation needs to be considered carefully because the outcomes are not always as apparent as they might

INTERPRETATION OF THE BIORHYTHM CONDITIONS

seem. The only really effective way of interpreting the biorhythm conditions and the way in which they might affect you, is by personal experience. As you become more familiar with the effects and the causes that they can have, you will find it easier to understand and react to the situations that prevail. Biorhythmic knowledge will enable you to deal far better with the problems or challenges that exist. Of course it is not possible to alter the biorhythm condition that is affecting you at a given point in time, but it is possible to compensate for any weaknesses that may exist in your cycles that could affect the way you perform or approach any particular problem or event.

This new found ability will often open new areas of potential that before were simply being missed. If, for example, you are in an emotionally low phase, it is possible, regardless of your other two cycle conditions, that you may not feel like getting involved in anything at all. However, being aware of your biorhythm condition in periods such as these can then show you clearly that you could well be suited to many tasks that require your other attributes. Rather than sitting indoors on a Saturday afternoon not really feeling in the mood for anything you might find that you would be better suited to reading a good book or even getting your tracksuit on and going out for a healthy jogging session. It is worth making these points because we have found from experience that the pleasure to be gained from finding that you are well suited to activities like this, instead of just sitting around, is very satisfying.

It is often a very useful idea to keep a personal record of your moods and feelings independently of your biorhythm conditions, so that you can relate how you actually feel and perform during the course of a month to your biorhythm chart. This blind diary process will enable you to see how in tune you are to your actual biorhythm cycle. To help with this we have prepared a blank Blind Diary section in Chapter 5. As biorhythm is a personal science and the strengths and effects of its conditions will be different in everybody it is important that you find yourself within the science. The guides that biorhythm offers are accurate but it is the power of its effects on you as an individual which will influence your response to future biorhythm advice.

To interpret the 27 main biorhythm permutations without any real personal experience is obviously going to be very difficult. The basic individual categories are simple enough to understand on their own and the complexity that arises when you study them as a group is only made more difficult when studied within the context of different external situations. In these cases it is a question of trying to understand what demands a particular situation will place upon an individual and then trying to predict how the prevailing biorhythm condition will affect the outcome. To achieve any real degree of accuracy you have to become familiar with aspects such as how naturally capable an individual is and what challenges or demands the particular situation will put on them. When this type of interpretation is placed upon biorhythm there are a number of uses to which the science can be put. For example, if you are looking at the biorhythm condition of two people who are going to be involved in a major debate on television or two sportsmen in a competition, it is possible to actually get some 'inside information' on the outcome. Results in these studies cannot of course be guaranteed but statistically you will improve the odds in predicting potential outcomes. But before you all rush down to the local betting shop to try out the theory it is important to note that very careful analysis is required to get the right result.

The sensible way to deal with any warnings that biorhythm may point out is to be aware of your weaknesses and then to try and guard against leaving yourself open to the obvious mistakes that the situation may encourage. With continued use you will quickly find yourself almost subconsciously aware of where you are in your particular cycles, much the same as your ability to estimate the time of day without looking at your watch. However, it is important to not let the biorhythm conditions govern your life to such an extent that you will not be prepared to tackle any task if you are not biorhythmically suited to it. Biorhythm should be treated as an extra tool to achieving your best; after all, you have managed to get through life so far without the aid of this book. Biorhythm should be regarded as something that can give you the extra edge, or point out times when caution should be observed.

Another area that needs to be carefully controlled is the mental influence that biorhythm may place upon you. If, for example, you find that you may not be biorhythmically suited to a particular activity then it is all too easy to feel that your performance will suffer badly as a result. This is not always the case as many things in which we participate during life are well within our normal capabilities regardless of what our biorhythm condition is, and it is important to differentiate between what could be termed challenging and what is second nature. If you follow this rule then it is likely that you will get the best out of the science without becoming one of its patients.

THE BIORHYTHM PHASES

There are 27 main permutations that can exist between the three biorhythm categories and each one of these can last from a minimum of a day through to 11 days depending on the position of each cycle at the time. The following guide will help you to see what can be expected from the 27 phases, but this information should be used only as an initial guide until you have adapted the phases to suit you best. This will become apparent as your experience with the science increases.

P E I

+ + +

Days don't come better than this! Physically, emotionally and intellectually you are at your best. You should try to maximise your efforts fully to realise your potential and push achievements to a new level.

PEI

+ + −

Today should be a good positive day for you. Your physical and emotional highs will encourage you to tackle anything. Careful consideration should be given to the negative intellectual cycle position to avoid problems during this charged up period.

+ − +

You may experience a feeling of depression today. If this is the case utilise your intellectual sharpness and physical strengths to turn this into a good constructive day to maximise opportunity.

+ − −

Think before you act today. Because of the emotional and intellectual lows in your cycle your capacity for rational thought is below par. This is a good time for exercise and sporting activity so try to capitalise on your physical high.

− + +

Physically you are unlikely to perform at your best today. However, the positive effects of your emotional and intellectual cycles should leave you feeling both creative and perceptive. This a good opportunity to push yourself forward on matters that require mental application, as you should be sharper than usual.

− + −

Being both physically and intellectually low you may not feel inclined to cut a leading edge today. Take stock of your situation and give yourself a chance to recharge. This is a good time to use your emotional positive phase to generate new ideas and socialise with friends.

− − +

Today is best spent with intellectual pursuits, so try to avoid any tricky physical or emotional situations if you can. Although you may feel down and depressed your ability for clear thought is at a very good stage, so let this see you through the day.

− − −

This is very much a day to stay calm and take it easy. Although you may well feel low and in a negative mood, it is important to remember that this is only a temporary phase and things will improve shortly. It is also important to be aware of the fact that during this phase you are well below your best so operate with caution.

PEI

+ + C

A good day physically and emotionally with plenty of energy and positive feelings. It would, however, be wise to make an effort today to control your decision-making, especially in matters of judgement, to avoid the possibility of any accidents.

+ − C

Physically you should feel strong today. You need to guard against your emotional low but great care is needed on intellectual matters to safeguard yourself against a serious error of judgement.

+ C +

A good day for you to enjoy any physical or intellectual activity, with plenty of energy and perspective. Please consider any emotional situations very carefully, as lack of concentration can lead to mishaps!

+ C −

Despite your physical high today your emotions are at a critical stage, and this is not helped by your intellectual negative capability. Avoid preoccupation in order to get you through this day without incident.

− + C

Let your emotional position dominate today. Although you may well be feeling physically drained and intellectually unstable your positive mood should lift you. You must however be prepared for unexpected hazards and guard against mistakes.

− − C

Today is a day for taking things easy and you may feel short of stamina and drive. Your intellectual instability will necessitate careful thought when considering important decisions. It is important to bear this in mind in risky situations.

− C +

You may well feel drained and emotionally somewhat down in the dumps today, but because of your intellectual prowess you should attend to important matters that require thought. Attention to detail will help to guard against accidents.

− C −

This is not a good day. You could seriously be lacking in stamina and sharpness and this, combined with your critical emotional cycle, will leave you exposed to dangers that you would normally avoid. Tread with caution!

P E I

C + +

Your physical critical condition may well leave you feeling shaky and out of balance, so use the positive aspects of your emotional and intellectual cycles to help increase your perception of dangerous situations.

C + −

Use the favourable effect of your emotional cycle to overcome the unstable physical feeling that you may be experiencing. The fact that you are also intellectually low may leave you open to mishaps so take care.

C − +

Physically tired and emotionally low you may feel depressed with only your intellectual high to compensate. In this condition you are exposed and should take care not to lose clarity and ignore your intellectual assets.

C − −

Having both emotional and intellectual lows could well leave your capacity for clear thought severely limited and this, coupled with a critical physical condition, could leave you open to hazards. It is important to operate with caution.

+ C C

Your physical high should give strength and staying power today. Emotionally and intellectually you are at a critical stage and this could leave you feeling uninspired and somewhat mixed up. Guard against the nature of this high risk day!

− C C

Physically you could feel drained today. Please note that your emotional and intellectual critical conditions require you to take care with decisions and matters of judgement. Move cautiously on this highly precarious day.

C + C

Having a physical critical combined with the same intellectual condition could throw your bodily coordination badly out of balance leaving you open to all kinds of danger. Make use of your emotional resources today.

C − C

The double critical in both your physical and intellectual cycles could leave you feeling unsteady both in body and mind. A depressed emotional state is not going to make this an enjoyable day and you need to take care to avoid any potentially dangerous situations.

P E I

C C +

A pent up and anxious feeling could well affect your behaviour today. However, you should try to capitalise on your positive intellectual strengths to avert any rash or dangerous actions. An awkward day.

C C –

Today may feel like a major uphill struggle as you could well be experiencing a feeling of disharmony and lethargy. Being understandably off the pace, situations that require rapid response may catch you out!

C C C

Well, this is it. **TRIPLE CRITICAL!** If it's going to happen it could well be today. If you can't stay in bed, extreme caution must be observed in every avenue during this highly hazardous day. Be lucky!

3

BIORHYTHM AND OTHER PEOPLE

For as long as the science of biorhythm has existed its followers have been keen to make biorhythmic comparisons between two or more individuals, this comparison being commonly known as biorhythm compatibility. When this is considered it is important to not make what may seem obvious assumptions. For example, if two individuals were studying the same university degree course and shared similar leisure interests, onlookers would quite rightly describe the two people as having compatible intellectual pursuits, although biorhythmically they may actually only be a few per cent compatible! Biorhythm does not attempt to find intellectually compatible people by studying their individual intellectual pursuit, it is concerned with the comparison of their respective 33-day intellectual cycles. What biorhythm compatibility really refers to is how synchronous the people in question are with one another when comparing their respective biorhythm positions. This comparison can be made across all three biorhythm cycles to form an overall compatibility picture.

Biorhythm compatibility is not intended to distract individuals from applying biorhythm at a personal level, it is intended to act as a supplement to understanding how biorhythm conditions interact between two or more people. In any given situation one should look first to how biorhythm can be used for the job in hand and then to the people involved, taking into account their respective biorhythm conditions.

Determining shared day percentages for two or more people is a fairly straightforward calculation. You need to begin by establishing how many days apart the people concerned were born. Once this has been calculated it is simply a question of dividing that number by the respective cycle lengths to find out

Days Apart in Cycle	PHYSICAL		EMOTIONAL		INTELLECTUAL	
	SHARED DAYS Out of 23	%	SHARED DAYS Out of 28	%	SHARED DAYS Out of 33	%
0	23	100	28	100	33	100
1	21	91	26	93	31	94
2	19	83	24	86	29	88
3	17	74	22	79	27	82
4	15	65	20	71	25	76
5	13	57	18	64	23	70
6	11	48	16	57	21	64
7	9	39	14	50	19	58
8	7	30	12	43	17	52
9	5	22	10	36	15	46
10	3	13	8	29	13	39
11	1	4	6	21	11	33
12	1	4	4	14	9	27
13	3	13	2	7	7	21
14	5	22	0	0	5	15
15	7	30	2	7	3	9
16	9	39	4	14	1	3
17	11	48	6	21	1	3
18	13	57	8	29	3	9
19	15	65	10	36	5	15
20	17	74	12	43	7	21
21	19	83	14	50	9	27
22	21	91	16	57	11	33
23	23	100	18	64	13	39
24			20	71	15	46
25			22	79	17	52
26			24	86	19	58
27			26	93	21	64
28			28	100	23	70
29					25	76
30					27	82
31					29	88
32					31	94
33					33	100

Table of Shared Day Percentages

how many days apart in each cycle the individuals are. The following example illustrates the technique involved.

Janet was born on 1 January 1970.
John was born on 1 November 1969.

Therefore John is 61 days older than Janet.

Physical compatibility: $61 \div 23 = 2$ remainder 15 (days apart)
Emotional compatibility: $61 \div 28 = 2$ remainder 5 (days apart)
Intellectual compatibility: $61 \div 33 = 1$ remainder 28 (days apart)

Shared day ratings for Janet and John are as follows:

Physical   30%
Emotional   64%
Intellectual   70%

These shared day ratings are applicable on a consistent basis, because John will always be 61 days older than Janet their percentages will not change.

PERSONAL RELATIONSHIPS

If you are a single person and looking for a prospective partner to spend the rest of your life with it can seem to be an extremely daunting task to find someone that matches up to your ideal mental image of what he or she should be. This often leads one to feel the common emotion of 'I'll never find the person I'm looking for'.

Relationships are many and varied but when it comes to studying the theoretical compatibility between them it is by no means uncommon to find a rating that is entirely unexpected. Love is a powerful and little understood force; what couples see in each other can't always be seen by people outside of the relationship. During the course of most people's lives they will find a partner to settle down with, the usual basis for their choice being influenced by a combination of such factors as physical attraction, sharing similar interests and common activities. Contrary to popular belief it can be quite easy to find a partner, but what is difficult is making sure it is someone with whom you will want to spend the rest of your life.

A successful relationship will stand the test of time if there is a common harmony between the partners, although there are many cases of people staying together even when they clearly do not get on very well all of the time. Some people are prepared to accept this situation and carry on in the relationship regardless, often for the sake of their children or because they believe that their relationship is no better or worse than many others and is therefore something to be put up with. What may have started as a physical relationship can deteriorate as the attraction between the people becomes more distant and jaded, and it is at this point that the underlying differences in personalities and interests will come to the fore. Physical attraction needs to be backed up by a significantly stronger bond and it is within this context that biorhythm can be employed.

Getting Physical

Biorhythm compatibility between people can be used not only as a guiding hand in the quest for a successful relationship, but it can also offer ongoing assistance to the forces at work within the relationship on a day-to-day basis. Understanding the effects of compatibility within the framework of a relationship is quite straightforward once the actual calculations have been performed. A high level of physical compatibility, anything over 65 per cent, means that for most of the time the couple will share the same ups and downs. This presents them with an opportunity to plan or take part in physically related activities, such as going for walks in the countryside. If they can coincide the time of their outing to ensure that both of their physical rhythms are favourable (an easy task within this particular relationship) then they will be rewarded with an enjoyable day out as both will be in an excellent position for undertaking such an activity. This application of biorhythm can be repeated in many different avenues, and once used and benefited from the incentive is there to continue looking for further common ground through biorhythm study.

A common problem faced by people who are ignorant of biorhythm influence is the irritation they feel when they want to begin something new, like an exercise programme, with their partner, but the idea is met with a lukewarm response. It would be better to check one's partner's biorhythm chart to discover whether they are undergoing a physically and emotionally negative period before suggesting anything new and strenuous.

Emotional compatibility needs to be approached from a different perspective to that of physical compatibility within a relationship. Here it is certainly not a case of 'the higher the better' when it comes to look at the actual compatibility percentage, as a strong relationship needs a certain amount of debate and differences in approach if is not to stagnate and lack spice. If in a relationship, the partners have 100 per cent emotional shared days, the couple would be in the best, worst and critical moments at exactly the same time. Of course we are not suggesting that they should be diametrically opposed either; what is called for is a good balance or spread of the highs and lows. This would enable the relationship to cater for one person being a little down in the dumps by the other being on an emotional upswing, thus lifting the general mood to a mutually pleasant level. A figure of about 50% would be good as this offers enough variation to prevent the relationship becoming stale while still allowing for plenty of time when similar moods and enthusiams are shared.

Heart of the Matter

Thought Waves

The intellectual cycle is also not at its best when the couple share the same condition for 100 per cent of the time, as this can lead to things going a bit stale. Couples with a high percentage of shared days will, however, display an uncannily similar attitude to dealing with problems and will tend to home in on similar solutions. These couples will tend to be great talkers and can be found discussing ideas and problems into the small hours of the morning. A balanced shared day percentage when considering the intellectual cycle is around 80 per cent, as this will keep the partners basically in tune with one another with the odd day when differences can be expressed, which will lead to a more balanced relationship. Relationships that have a fairly low shared day percentage will not find it easy to talk about fresh topics and different subjects as it will be rare for both of them to have an inclination to do so.

The relevant importance of intellectual compatibility will vary with the many different types of relationships that exist today, being far more appropriate in some than in others. Couples who enjoy a close relationship which is not based on each other's intellectual capabilities will find that its importance is limited, but for those relationships that are centred around intellectual pursuits and activities, then it is much more important that they should share a good level of intellectual compatibility.

In summary, when discussing biorhythm compatibility in the context of personal relationships, what is needed is a sense of balance and proportion. Biorhythm cannot offer absolute rules to be followed for success as it does not take into account external influences that may have an effect on the situation. It is for the people concerned to take the time out to compare their own biorhythm condition and its compatibility with their own circumstances and needs. Studying biorhythm can help explain why trivial arguments can sometimes develop into open conflict. Biorhythm information will allow you to make adjustments to your daily outlook and perceptions with the aim of avoiding the unnecessary and increasing the harmonious. It takes patience and

	PHYSICAL	EMOTIONAL	INTELLECTUAL
BOTH POSITIVE	Both parties have energy and stamina. A good time for joint jobs such as decorating, gardening etc. Also good for joint leisure activities.	Both being confident and creative should lend itself to discussing new ideas, choosing home furnishings/decorations and throwing parties.	A good time for discussion and understanding each other's needs. Both parties should have a clear head with plenty of perspective and an ability to communicate effectively.
ONE POSITIVE ONE NEGATIVE	This situation can lead to friction, especially if the positive partner is keen to get physical and the negative partner will want to take it easy.	The negative partner can help keep the positive partner on the ground when creative ideas are flowing. The positive person can get frustrated, however, if the negative partner comes across as a wet blanket.	The negative partner may be suffering from memory lapse, absent mindedness and irrational thoughts, the best course of action for the positive partner is to act as an intellectual minder.
ONE POSITIVE ONE CRITICAL	This is a potentially dangerous situation if the positive partner is pushing their Critical partner to limits that could expose them to danger. It is particularly important to avoid any hazardous pursuits.	A similar situation to the one above except that the positive partner could quite unwittingly upset their Critical partner with forceful ideas and lots of creative energy.	The positive partner in this situation could end up not appreciating their partner's intellectual shortcomings. A particularly dangerous situation is where the positive partner is teaching the other to drive.
BOTH NEGATIVE	Both being less than eager to get involved in physical pursuits these periods are best spent taking it easy.	Being unemotional, introvert and cool-headed this is a good time for singular activity.	This a potentially worrying time with both parties being 'less than brilliant' at remembering important dates and times. A time to check with each other that important tasks are being attended to.
ONE NEGATIVE ONE CRITICAL	Both parties are reasonably compatible with the exception of one being prone to accidents. This is certainly a time for both to 'take it easy'.	This is a potentially fiery situation, particularly if there is friction in the relationship. The Critical person, who could be feeling insecure, could find their emotions being met with a lack of sympathy by their partner.	This is a similar situation to both being negative, however the Critical person may be let down by the negative partner when looking for help. This could lead to a feeling of that partner being unreliable.
BOTH CRITICAL	Critical days are bad enough on their own, but if you're both having one your resources to guard against accidents will be limited. Only those that are 100% compatible will experience this problem.	The Critical emotional day is one of getting flustered coupled with worries and anxieties. Awareness can help in leaning on each other instead of having heated and often petty arguments.	Both being prone to irrational thoughts and lack of logic could lead to a loss of communication in ideas and opinions. This could cause arguments, particularly if you are unaware of these conditions.

Table of Compatibility Conditions

a certain amount of sympathy to overcome difficult times but with biorhythm information you now have the ability to work towards a more fruitful coexistence.

The above table studies biorhythm compatibility amongst two people within a personal relationship. It is intended to illustrate the basic form of a compatibility comparison within biorhythm and to offer some explanation of how different conditions between partners can affect the relationship. As with personal biorhythm it is a question of looking at the overall picture and not at each cycle individually, so the explanation given can be further enhanced by considering the other cycles' positions for the people in question. For example, if both parties were experiencing an emotional critical but were opposed intellectually, then the picture could be affected. In a highly charged emotional scene with both parties feeling a little hurt and insecure it could be the intellectually positive partner that keeps the situation under control.

Putting It Together

The one aspect of biorhythm compatibility that should be understood is that to calculate an overall compatibility rating it is not simply a case of adding the three individual percentages and dividing them by three to find an average. The reasoning behind this is simple: only the physical cycle can be summarised as being 'the higher the better' when referring to shared day percentage, as the emotional and intellectual cycles do not follow this pattern. If, for example, two people were born on the same date they would have a 100 per cent shared day percentage in all three cycles, but this would not make them overall 100 per cent compatible because the emotional optimum is around 50 per cent and the intellectual optimum is around 80 per cent.

The most mathematically accurate way of determining an overall biorhythm compatibility is to compare the actual shared day percentage with the optimum shared day percentage and then calculate how far away in each case the particular calculation is from the optimum. The physical cycle comparison does not require this calculation because its optimum is 100 per cent and therefore any other percentage is directly proportional to it. When we consider the emotional cycle the optimum is 50 per cent so the compatibility rating should be expressed as a percentage away from the optimum. If, for example, a couple have a 75 per cent shared day percentage then their overall compatibility would be calculated as being halfway between the best percentage (50 per cent) and the worst percentage (100 per cent) making them 50 per cent emotionally compatible. This calculation applies to emotional shared day percentages below 50 per cent in the same way, the only difference being that the worst percentage is 0 per cent instead of 100 per cent.

Dealing with all these different percentages can be daunting, a more accessible method is to refer to the actual number of shared days instead of their percentages. The example below shows how this overall rating has been arrived at.

Cycle	Number of Days Apart in Cycle	Number of Shared Days	Optimum Number of Shared Days	Number of Days Away From Optimum	Away From Optimum as a Percentage	Actual Biorhythmic Compatibility
Physical	15	7	23	16	70	100% − 70% = 30%
Emotional	5	18	14	4	29	100% − 29% = 71%
Intellectual	28	23	25	2	8	100% − 8% = 92%

The three final compatibility percentages shown above are calculated with respect to the optimum in each case and we can use the average of the three to represent an overall compatibility rating which in this case is 30 + 71 + 92 = 193. If we divide this figure of 193 by 3 we will get the overall percentage (to the nearest whole number), therefore Janet and John are overall 64 per cent biorhythmically compatible.

PARENTAL CARE

The relationship that exists between child and parent is a close and vitally important one. The nature of that relationship is dependent upon a number of separate issues such as the levels of happiness and security a child feels, as well as the amount and standard of guidance they receive.

Children do not generally have as highly developed a sense of awareness as their parents. This is mainly because of a lack of experience of the different situations that life has in store for us all, meaning that children have to rely much more on their own instincts when in situations they have not experienced before, leaving them open to mistakes and the possible dangers that worry all parents. Due to this lack of experience on the part of children, biorhythm plays a stronger role in their ups and downs, strengths and weaknesses up to the age of about eleven than it does in older children and adults. The positive side to this predicament is that adults now have the ability to use biorhythm to improve the way in which their children develop and can guard them more closely when they are in a vulnerable period.

This improvement can be effected in a number of ways. For example, when a child is undergoing a critical day and asks to go out to play with some friends in the park it is possible to warn the child that this is a particularly vulnerable day and to be extra careful. If, however, that is the full extent of parental application of biorhythm theory then it is extremely unlikely that it will bear much fruit because the child will not understand what is being said and why, and will be much less likely to take any note of it. But, if the same parent was to offer a more balanced understanding of biorhythm and the reasons for its use then they would be much more likely to see the advice being acted upon.

The Learning Curve

How, then, is it possible to give this more balanced understanding to children? The way to achieve the greatest understanding of biorhythm and derive the maximum benefit is to begin when the child is at the 'early learning' stage. A good starting point is to use the study of your child's biorhythm condition to pre-determine an intellectually positive phase which is best suited to work of a learning nature. During this period the child's mind will be bright, clear and able to absorb new information quickly and easily. This is a great confidence builder for children as they can see with their own eyes how simple it can be to begin studying. If you combine the intellectual position with an emotionally positive period as well, the child actually becomes eager to start and continue studying. There has only been a limited amount of research in this area but it has been found that children are receptive to this kind of 'play' from the age of about eighteen months.

With continued application of this information it is possible for children to achieve quite extraordinary results. By the age of four it is possible for a child to be able to read, write, count to a hundred and learn arithmetic tables with ease. If used in a structured manner, biorhythm can give a child a much better start in primary education and in life itself. It is at the early stage of learning that one is most receptive and responsive to new thinking, so it is here that a parent should begin a child's education in the science of biorhythm.

Household Harmony

We have looked briefly at applying biorhythm theory to the development of a child's basic education and how they might be able to resolve some of the mysteries that surround them. Now we should turn our attention to the day-to-day interaction or compatibility of families as a whole. Both parents and children alike can make use of knowing what the spread of biorhythm conditions is throughout the household. While growing up, children are bound to become temperamental at times and the way in which those around them react to this is important. There are two basic options: first, the unscientific one which is to tell the child to shut up and stop behaving in a spoilt manner, and secondly, there is a more reasoned approach which is to study the child's biorhythm condition and see if it holds any pointers to what is going on. For example, parents are well advised to keep an advance note of when their child will experience an emotionally critical day, as it is on these days that they are more prone to flare-ups. An interesting point to note is when a child is behaving in an abnormally hyperactive state, you should not be surprised if you find them undergoing the influence of a triple positive. In later life these energies will be channelled into more constructive activities.

Advance warning allows parents to try to avoid situations that may spark off problems. This does not mean that parents have to start altering their lifestyle or pander to the whims of their children, but it can make for an open and productive relationship as opposed to a hostile and unproductive one. This learning process cuts both ways as it will help children to understand and accommodate the less than perfect actions to which even the best parents are prone from time to time.

The main issue of a parent to child relationship is that of understanding. If both the child and the parent are able to understand what makes people behave the way they do, then it is a short step to overcoming the barriers in trying to resolve traditional problems. Without biorhythm guidance on this matter it is all too easy to find shortcut reasons that explain neither why these problems occur, nor what can be done to help.

SPORTING ARENAS

Biorhythm plays an important role in many aspects of sporting life and is especially useful in deciding whether a particular team or individual is likely to shine at a sporting event. It is first of all necessary to identify which of the three cycles are key to the success of that particular sport, as each sport places a different set of requirements on biorhythm compatibility.

Broadly speaking, it is a matter of common sense to think through what are the likely combinations of biorhythm positions that will be favourable or otherwise to the sport in question. It is clear that some sports are going to be influenced more directly by strong physical cycle conditions as opposed to favourable emotional or intellectual ones and of course the reverse will also apply. So how does one determine which of the cycles is important and what type of overall mix would be most beneficial?

Team Spirit

To begin with we will look at a team game situation, which gives the added consideration of how to determine which team members will benefit most from sharing a good level of biorhythm compatibility in order that the team can perform at its best. To help answer this question it is useful to choose a sport as a basis for study, beginning with an evaluation of what makes for a winning team in that particular field. It is not enough for the management to buy a number of star players to fill the team, as to be effective they will need consistently to display the qualities of organisation, discipline and motivation. If we look at a soccer team we will see that there are eleven players who are responsible for separate tasks within the team structure, and within this structure we must find which biorhythm conditions affect certain aspects of the team's performance.

It is not always the case, especially in *team* games, that the best possible position for all players is that of triple positive as this can lead individual players to become more interested in their own performance than that of the the team as a whole. However, the possibility of this happening for all eleven players is remote, as there are, after all, 27 different biorhythm permutations.

If we begin our study of biorhythm with the physical cycle, the team's power house, it should be noted that to be part of the team each player will already have taken part in an ongoing training programme in an effort to keep himself match fit, as well as practising his game skills. So to a certain extent we can take a good level of physical ability as read, although even in this area of a team's preparation biorhythm can offer the coach a good guide for when to push the training programme harder to get the most out of favourable conditions. However, he may decide to keep key players on light training duties if they are undergoing a physically negative period in order to avoid the dangers of possible strains and injuries. So, in which players is the physical cycle especially important? As the last line of defence the team's goalkeeper requires lightning fast reflexes and good overall agility to keep the ball out of the net, and these characteristics have been found to correlate very closely to the physical rhythm, being swiftest during the peak of the cycle and noticeably slower throughout the cycle's negative period. Those players who perform the greatest physical tasks during a game, the wingers and attackers, who are faced with a challenge requiring a good turn of speed and excellent timing on the ball will tend to be faster and more coordinated when their physical cycle position is positive.

As we have said soccer players already benefit from their physical training, but what of their emotional disposition during a game? Despite this being equally important to any successful team there is no training programme to cover this vital area. When looking at the emotional cycle in the context of the team game we will see that it has many subtle yet far-reaching effects on behaviour and performance. What makes the emotional cycle so vital to team performance and, therefore, very interesting to study, is that it governs the level of determination and inspiration that a player will put into his game performance, which in sporting terms could easily be the difference between winning and losing. A good positive position in the emotional cycle will see players in a confident, creative and determined mood. Combine this with favourable positions in the other two cycles and you have a recipe for a truly inspired 'man of the match' performance. However, it is not always good for the emotional cycle to be in its most positive form as this often brings with it cases of over-confidence, a particular problem if the overall biorhythm condition is not supported by complimentary positions in the other two cycles. For example, if a goalkeeper was in an emotionally positive condition yet he was also experiencing physical and intellectual negatives, then he could very easily fall into the trap of being too confident in his own abilities. This could lead to some very embarrassing situations, for instance poor reflexes at critical moments such as penalties and corners, or not giving situations that require careful judgement, like the positioning of the defence during free kicks, their full consideration. This said, the creative aspect of a positive and rising emotional cycle should not be underestimated, especially when looking at players who are involved in the 'set piece' type of game play which is vital to executing goal scoring moves. It is important to have belief in one's ability and if one can structure this facet within the team by ensuring a good level of emotional compatibility then clearly the players will operate better together.

A point worth noting is that the temperament of the players in a game situation can become highly charged, matching that of the spectators, and this could lead to irrational outbursts on the field with unfortunate consequences for player and team alike. This is especially important when a team is taking part in a knock-out or challenge format, for if a player loses his cool early on the team could face having to play without their star striker or defender. So team managers have to exercise caution when selecting players for this type of game if they are undergoing an emotional peak or, even worse, an emotionally critical day.

All managers would like their team to follow the game plan that he has calculated for them and it is to the intellectual cycle that we must turn to understand the level of strategy and planning that the team will demonstrate when they are on the field. An effective and not too complicated way for the manager to ensure that his tactics are followed is in the careful selection of the key men in the team and to make sure that they, at the very least, are aware of the team's overall strengths and weaknesses as indicated by biorhythm. This knowledge may prove crucial in times of pressure.

We can see, with the study of biorhythm in the context of team sport, how the players' conditions will vary and what different responses are required to best suit the team's needs. However, there are some restrictions placed on the ultimate application of the science. For instance, a top line first team squad will usually have no more than twenty players in total to choose from so it is not always possible to find a suitable compatibility between all the players at one time if they are to play in their normal positions. A possible solution is that, as most players are capable of playing in two or three different positions, they could be moved about the field in the light of their biorhythm condition to make the best use of their capabilities.

Whatever the situation, if biorhythm information is to offer the team good advice that will be acted upon, then it is necessary for the team to be made aware that the management is using it. This will help them to appreciate the subtleties of their own situation and the decisions that the manager might take as a result. A better understanding of what makes the body tick is something that should be shared for the common benefit of the squad. It will make it easier for players to accept tough decisions and encourage a team spirit to help members undergoing a vulnerable period.

One On One

Studying biorhythm for application to individual sportsmen/ women rather than on a team sport basis reduces significantly its complexity. The first step in using biorhythm to predict or give an insight into the potential result of a particular occasion or confrontation is to weigh up any external factors not directly related to biorhythm theory. This means that, first of all, one should give consideration to details such as past record, current form, the level of pre-event preparation and whether the competitors have met at this or any other venue before. This process is no different to that used by betting shops and casinos alike, as it is how they would calculate the betting odds. The obvious move is to bet on the favourite for the occasion, as all things being equal they are the most likely to win. However, biorhythm can be used to determine those occasions when all things are not equal; with 27 possible permutations, it is unlikely that both competitors should have similar biorhythm conditions.

As the effects of biorhythm are subtle and can be seen as indicators of an individual's capabilities or performance potential for any given day, it is unlikely that the effects can be measured when looking at a competition between a first-year novice and a multiple world championship winner. For example, it is unlikely that Stefan Edberg, despite being under the influence of very poor biorhythm conditions, should be defeated in the first round by a novice with very strong biorhythm conditions. The reason for such seeming invincibility against the prevailing biorhythm conditions is that one has to look at other factors such as form, playing surface and past record.

The Thinking Man's Competitor

A boxer preparing for an important fight can plan his pre-event preparation to make the best use of the time available. During his physically positive phase he can aim to complete a particularly vigorous stamina and strength programme which would make good use of his higher energy reserves and good recuperative powers, yet during his physically negative periods he could turn his attention to less strenuous matters such as tactics for the fight and publicity commitments.

When preparing for a fixed date, biorhythm gives one the opportunity to assess the relative strengths and weakness of the opposition. It is then a simple matter to plan the remaining pre-event training in conjunction with ongoing daily biorhythm conditions to make preparation really count towards the final result. For example, if a fighter was aware in advance that on the night of the fight he would be undergoing a physical negative and would suffer a loss of reflex speed, he would be able to include special reflex training in his overall programme, or indeed he may even be able to change his tactics to lessen the impact of this temporary problem. If his usual style of boxing is aggressive, it would obviously be wise for him to conserve energy so as not to be left short at the end. Without that insight he may find himself running out of steam in the later rounds, while the opponent remains untroubled by his efforts. It is this assessment of an individual's own condition and that of their opponents which will bear the greatest tactical fruits.

The study of sport using biorhythm is made more difficult when there is an extra link between the individual and the end result. An example of this is in motorsport, where the extra link is between man and machine. It is no longer a question of the driver being personally capable of racing to the finish, because if the car isn't capable of making it there, the driver's efforts will be wasted.

In motorsport the factors that govern the results are split between the driver and the car and thus all attempts at maximising performance need to take account of both aspects. A racing driver will feel the effects of biorhythm very strongly as he is involved in a challenging area of sport that is guaranteed to get the blood flowing and the adrenalin pumping, and this stressful situation makes for an extreme challenge to both mind and body. Successful use of biorhythm will enable a driver to analyse his personal abilities to a clinical level. This can prove a vital advantage in trying to develop a competitive performance as it will give a good indication of where to start looking for potential gains and losses. For example, if a car is lapping a circuit one second slower than it should, it is difficult to tell if the engine is missing a small amount of horsepower or whether the driver is simply having an off day. A quick look at the driver's biorhythm chart should soon give a point in the right direction.

During the race the driver will already be aware by pre-event study of his strengths and weaknesses for that day's competition.

He may also choose to study the biorhythm condition of his main rivals to see if there is any advantage to be gained or danger to be avoided. For example, his physical and emotional condition could be far superior to that of his competitors, allowing him to set a fast pace in the knowledge that he is in the best position to withstand the test of endurance, unlike his rivals. Also, if he has studied his opponents and observed that one of them was undergoing a critical on the day of the race he would be pre-warned to give that driver a very wide berth.

Safety in sport is always of paramount importance and here again biorhythm can offer some very real advice. For the driver, there are the obvious warnings against undue bravado, but for the mechanics who prepare the car there are also points to be looked at. An obvious one is to ensure that whilst undertaking work of a safety related nature, i.e. brakes or steering, one has a good level of patience, care and manual ability to carry out the work. This would ideally mean a positive physical and intellectual period with a lower-key emotional condition. An important point here is that one should try to match the job being done with the prevailing biorhythm conditions.

To be a true champion it is necessary to be in excellent physical condition, have a high degree of emotional motivation and a good measure of intellectual capacity to deal with matters of skill and tactics, but as always there needs to be a balance between the three to achieve the very best results. Biorhythm study can be undertaken in relation to all sports, but it is best suited to the ones that call for a high degree of commitment and those that challenge the competitor in the extreme.

COMMERCIAL LIFE

The world of business is a similar environment to that of sport, being fiercely competitive, with only a few places at the top reserved for the best performers. Biorhythm can influence and therefore be harnessed in most areas of business life, but requires a positive attitude to working with new concepts of commercial practice.

A common difficulty facing most organisations is the compatibility or lack of it in the worker to boss relationship. The manager or foreman in the workplace can often be seen as an exacting tyrant constantly hurrying for work to be completed straight away, exactly the way he wants it done. Biorhythm information provides a way to judge any individual situation independently of any personal differences, thereby reducing the number of needless arguments. It also means that, armed with this information, it is possible to take control of the direction you are moving in and actually to pre-plan and time manoeuvres to perfection. You may have a good idea which you believe should be taken up without delay. The best approach is to wait a moment and see when your boss will be in the best intellectual position to receive it. In the long run this is a far quicker and much more productive method than crashing about like a bull in a china shop only to catch someone in the wrong frame of mind and be turned away at point blank range. This can help to explain why you may find in the office environment, where there is little or no socialising outside of office hours, that certain people develop a close relationship with the boss while others do not.

New Beginnings

Even before beginning employment there is usually the dreaded interview to overcome and it is at this point that we should really begin to look into how biorhythm and business can operate well together. It is obviously extremely unlikely that you will be able to obtain your interviewer's date of birth information and consequently you will not be able to carry out any pre-emptive compatibility study. However, biorhythm can give sound advice as to your most favourable time to perform well and, therefore, the best time to make the appointment.

The best biorhythm condition depends on what type of job you are applying for. A good sprinkling of positive conditions is a promising start, although some vacancies require us to be at our very best in certain departments and decidedly less so in others. For example, in applying to be a marketing executive, then very high emotional and intellectual conditions are preferable as they will help to give the impression of good creative skills, clarity and precision. On the other hand, in applying for the position of air traffic controller, which calls for steady nerves and an ability to keep track of many details at once, then it would be wise to schedule the interview at the peak of the intellectual cycle, but with a more low-key emotional condition.

Horses For Courses

Another aspect of possible biorhythm use in business is the selective scheduling of jobs on a day-to-day basis. As we now know, everybody is more adept at particular duties at certain times than at others. So a department manager who is responsible for running a multi-function style workplace can employ biorhythm knowledge to improve productivity as well as keeping staff morale at a good level. This can be achieved by training the workforce for a variety of jobs and scheduling the duty rosta to match the prevailing biorhythm conditions of the staff to the demands that each separate job requires. For example, the front line of all companies is the receptionist who presents the first impression of the company to the general public, so cooperation, patience and efficiency are of paramount importance. The ideal biorhythm condition would be positive emotional and intellectual cycles while the physical condition is much less important.

If, however, the receptionist has a peaking physical cycle and is negative in the other two, it would be advisable to assign him or her less mentally demanding work instead of putting the person under any undue time pressure or in contact with potentially upsetting customers.

The possibilities are endless and simply require a small amount of thought and imagination during the first five minutes of the manager's day. Both the manager and the company will reap the rewards of improved service to the customer and a happier staff who will enjoy far more varied, interesting work.

Planning Ahead

The daily progression of the three cycles can be turned to special advantage when applied to certain types of work which may take days or even weeks to move from conception through to completion. For example, a computer programmer can take advantage of the cyclical nature of biorhythm by beginning the original thinking and mapping out of the design during an emotional cycle which is rising through the positive phase towards its peak. This brings the benefit of an increased capacity to generate original ideas at a time when creative and thought-provoking skills are best.

When it is time to sit down and write the software a good physical position is called for along with a favourable intellectual position. This will enable the programmer to work more quickly due to the clarity of thought brought on by a strong intellectual condition and more accurately and skilfully due to the positive condition of the physical cycle.

Playing It Safe

One of the major advantages of biorhythm is its ability to predict when we are significantly more likely to suffer a self-induced accident. It is on these single, double and triple critical days that we are at our most vulnerable. This has been known and understood for some time with a number of international consultancies spreading the word of accident prevention with the aid of biorhythm to companies in the United States, Japan and, to a lesser extent, in mainland Europe.

The first group attracted to the offerings of biorhythm were

Japanese transport companies in activities as diverse as taxi and bus operators and road and rail haulage contractors. Their interest originally centred around warning drivers at the start of the morning in question when they were undergoing a critical day. This produced an amazing 50 per cent reduction in accident rates, that was maintained throughout the following years despite the fact that the national incidence of road traffic accidents had increased during that same period. This type of preventative action has a beneficial knock-on effect, as the reduced accident rate brought similar reductions in the annual insurance premium. It soon became apparent that the reduction in accidents meant that their drivers and vehicles were spending far more time out on the road earning money and not in the workshops being repaired! The end result was a significant increase in profits.

Another aspect of biorhythm application in industry follows a similar theme to the traffic situation. In an engineering shop or manufacturing plant there are a number of machine-related jobs ranging from heavy duty pressings through to lathe work. These jobs call for a good level of accuracy but are extremely dangerous when operated carelessly. Here is a situation crying out for some advance warning of the lapses in concentration and reduced abilities brought on by a critical day in one of the three rhythms. Again, by careful planning, biorhythm stands to make a considerable contribution to industrial safety and improvements in efficiency.

Throughout the business world we can see how the application of biorhythm theory can offer gains in productivity and overall efficiency as well as boosting morale. This theory requires the understanding of straightforward principles and how they may be applied on a worker-by-worker, job-by-job basis. With a positive and imaginative approach it is possible to implement and benefit from biorhythm from the moment you become aware of its potential.

4

CELEBRITY BIORHYTHM

This chapter will look at a number of individual biorhythm case histories for well-known people, and will also study a number of famous partnerships and relationships. It is intended that these examples will help you to get a very visual understanding of the factors and influences that biorhythm can have on situations and circumstances surrounding the lives of the people concerned. A number of different biorhythm conditions and compatibility ratings are employed to make this section as comprehensive as possible.

The biorhythm examples featured in this chapter do not have a phase table included with them but feature a detailed explanation of the events that took place to serve as a historical reference. If you want to interpret the days leading up to or after the event in question you can refer to the 27 biorhythm condition explanations that are covered in Chapter 2. This may help you to study the example in greater detail by seeing what effect the days surrounding the event may have had in determining the final outcome.

The biorhythm calculator supplied with this book can be used to set up the examples included in this section, which will help to familiarise you with the techniques involved in getting the calculations correct. The compatibility reports contained in this section will, in certain instances, make reference to both overall and shared day ratings for the people concerned. This is because in some cases the rules governing compatibility need to placed within the context of either a loving relationship like a marriage, or a business relationship such as a comedy duo. These two types of partnership will often be influenced by different aspects of their compatibility ratings, in some cases what is not suitable for one type of relationship will work far better in another. A lot will depend on external influences and the effects that they may have on the partnership, as this can often make what would seem to be an ideal compatibility rating fail through situations like increased pressure or stress. The different types of biorhythm compatibility ratings that are applied to these examples can be found on the first and second page of each report. The figures on the first page of the report are not the overall rating figures, they simply indicate the shared day percentage that is enjoyed between the partnership. The figures on the second page of the report will indicate the overall ratings and will show how close the examples are to the ideal shared day rating.

You can also see how these compatibilities are produced by studying the section in Chapter 3 that deals with the calculations, and a further study on biorhythm compatibility can be found in Chapter 5. Once you have examined this series of examples you should be able to relate the effects that biorhythm has on certain events and circumstances to your own personal situation whether it is in the context of a relationship or of the day-to-day running of your life.

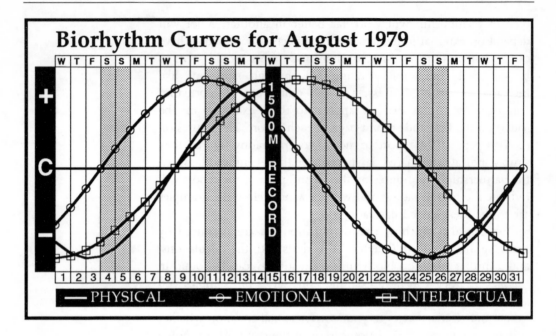

Biorhythm Curves for August 1979

— PHYSICAL   —⊖— EMOTIONAL   —⊟— INTELLECTUAL

SEBASTIAN COE

**d.o.b.
29 September
1956**

In terms of his running career the summer months of 1979 were certainly some of the most fruitful. In the weeks leading up to his 1500m World Record attempt on the night of 15 August, Coe had already secured both the 800m and mile World Records. Opinion at the time was varied as to whether or not Coe would do it; having gained two such important records it would have been understandable if his fitness was a little past its best.

Biorhythmically speaking, Coe could not have chosen a better time. His triple positive provided him with good strength, a positive attitude and a clear and organised head for race tactics. Coe put in a truly inspired performance which brought the Zurich crowd to its feet. As Coe passed the line he had secured his place in athletics history as the first man to hold three World Records simultaneously.

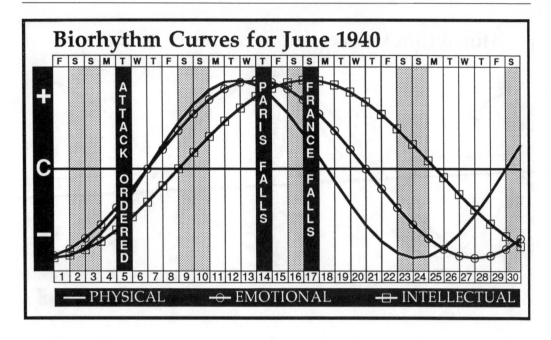

The 'blitzkrieg' of France in June 1940 was arguably Hitler's finest military hour. When he ordered the attack on 5 June he was only a few days away from entering the most powerful biorhythmic condition, the triple positive. Hitler's personal attention to the military effort was always with an eye for detail, so his biorhythmic conditions are worth considering when studying the overall tactics and methods used to further his infamous plans.

By 14 June the rapidly advancing German Army had captured Paris with Hitler at the peak of his biorhythmic triple. The 17th saw Petain, the French leader, asking Hitler for surrender terms. In true Hitler style the French signed the armistice in the same train and the same forest that saw the German surrender of 1918.

ADOLF HITLER

d.o.b.
20 April
1889

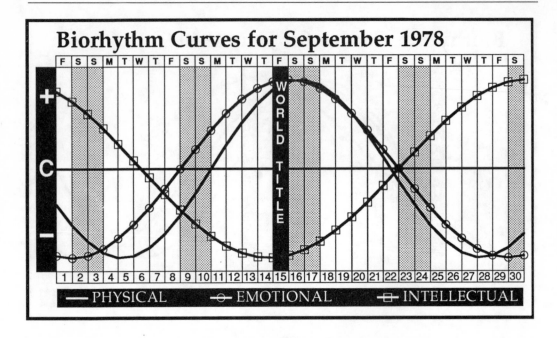

Biorhythm Curves for September 1978

— PHYSICAL   —○— EMOTIONAL   —⊟— INTELLECTUAL

MUHAMMED ALI

**d.o.b.
17 January
1942**

Muhammed Ali recaptured the World Heavyweight title by defeating George Foreman in October 1974 and went on to defend the title successfully on ten occasions. This run came to an abrupt end when he fought Leon Spinks on 15 February 1978. His biorhythm conditions at that time were physically critical and emotionally negative resulting in a defeat that shocked the world.

A rematch was scheduled for 15 September 1978 and on this occasion Ali's biorhythm conditions were in good enough shape for him to recapture the title. Our research into boxing has shown that a fighter's performance is more strongly linked to his physical and emotional conditions, and on this particular evening Ali's condition could not have been better. At his comparatively veteran age of 37, Ali won the title for a record third time.

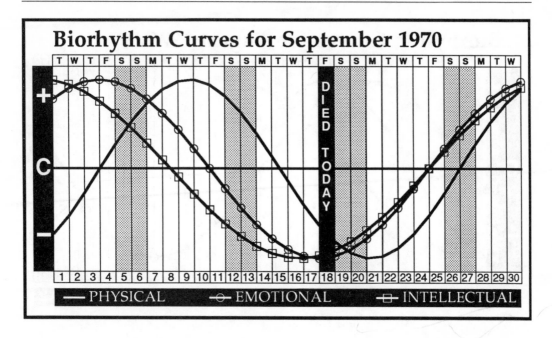

The early death of rock legend Jimi Hendrix robbed the world of one of its finest guitarists, though the circumstances surrounding his death are still unclear. Whether or not Hendrix committed suicide is still a matter of conjecture. The doctor's report at the time indicated that no trace of heroin was found in his body, although a considerable quantity of alcohol and barbiturates were, but there is no way of knowing whether he intended to take a lethal dose. His biorhythmn conditions are interesting from two points: first, that at the time he was undergoing a triple negative, a far more likely time for despair or depression, and secondly, if he had not intended to kill himself, his body was not in good enough shape to fight the influx of drink and pills. No-one will ever known what was going through his mind on that day, but biorhythm at least offers a feasible explanation.

JIMI HENDRIX

**d.o.b.
27 November
1942**

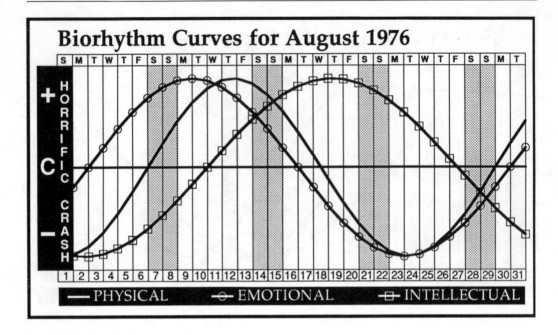

Biorhythm Curves for August 1976

—— PHYSICAL   —o— EMOTIONAL   —⊞— INTELLECTUAL

NICKI LAUDA

**d.o.b.
22 February
1949**

Nicki Lauda's motor racing career will not only be remembered for his World Championship successes but for his courage in returning to the track following his horrific crash at the German Grand Prix in 1976. Lauda, the World Champion at the time, sustained terrible burns and was lucky to get away with his life. His biorhythm condition on his near fatal day were far from ideal, being negative in all three rhythms, so even a driver of Lauda's stature would have been at less than his best. His physical and intellectual negatives are the most interesting because these would have affected his reflexes and his ability for clear and accurate thought.

The great man of motor racing returned to the sport and took up where he left off to continue his career, winning many more races and the World Championship in 1977 and 1984.

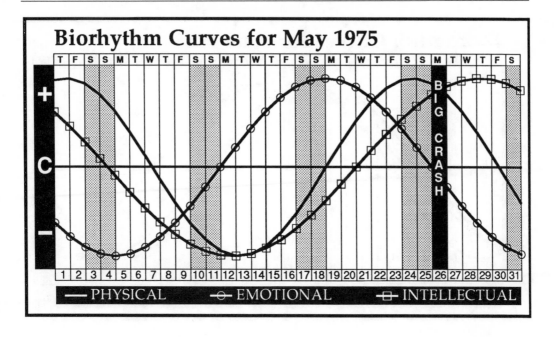

Biorhythm Curves for May 1975

| T | F | S | S | M | T | W | T | F | S | S | M | T | W | T | F | S | S | M | T | W | T | F | S | S | M | T | W | T | F | S |

1 2 3 4 5 6 7 8 9 10 11 12 13 14 15 16 17 18 19 20 21 22 23 24 25 26 27 28 29 30 31

BIG CRASH

—— PHYSICAL   ⊶ EMOTIONAL   ⊟ INTELLECTUAL

Evel Knievel was, in his day, one of the best entertainers in the stunt world. His antics on a motorcycle earned him fame and wealth across the world. He suffered a number of accidents during his career but was, on the whole, a true professional who tried to minimise the risks wherever possible. On 26 May 1975, however, Knievel was attempting to jump 13 buses on his motorcycle in front of a huge and expectant audience in England. The jump went badly wrong and Knievel suffered spinal injuries that were to put him out of action for many months. His critical emotional condition on the day may have affected his confidence or caused him to be in two minds right up until the point of the jump. This was, from a biorhythmic viewpoint, a very bad day to attempt such a stunt. Had he known his condition it is possible that this usually cautious man would have cancelled the attempt.

EVEL KNIEVEL

**d.o.b.
17 October
1938**

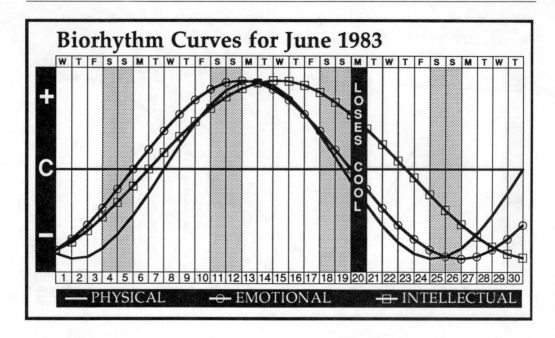

Biorhythm Curves for June 1983

— PHYSICAL   —o— EMOTIONAL   —⊟— INTELLECTUAL

JOHN McENROE

**d.o.b.
16 February
1959**

John McEnroe, the American tennis player with a reputation for losing his cool, really lost his temper on the first day of the 1983 Wimbledon Championships in England. McEnroe argued heatedly with the umpire and reeled off a string of abuse that very nearly got him disqualified from the tournament. His temperament is normally a fiery one but on this particular day, as he was undergoing an emotional critical, the umpire may well have benefited from knowing that McEnroe was even more likely to lose his cool. The pressure of being a top player who would lose everything if defeated in the first round provided an ideal situation to make this emotional condition surface with such venom.

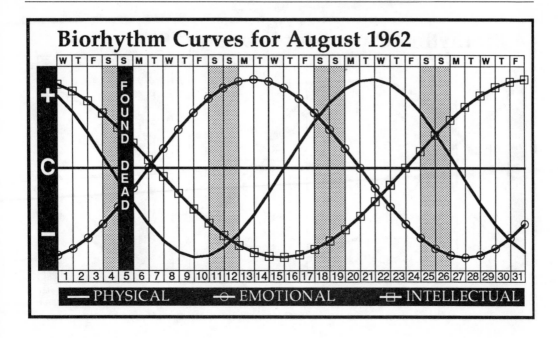

Biorhythm Curves for August 1962

PHYSICAL — EMOTIONAL — INTELLECTUAL

Marilyn Monroe's unique and often troubled life was brought to an untimely end on 5 August 1962. The exact circumstances surrounding her 'suicide' are still unclear and various theories have been put forward to try to explain what happened. Irrespective of the many possible outside sources that may have contributed to her death, a closer understanding of what Marilyn herself was going through at the time can be reached by studying her biorhythm condition. Marilyn had been emotionally negative for the previous 10 days and had recently passed through a physical critical. It is conceivable that her recent intellectual positive phase, providing her with the ability for clear thought, led her to believe that this was the only way out of the confusion in her life.

MARILYN MONROE

d.o.b. 1 June 1926

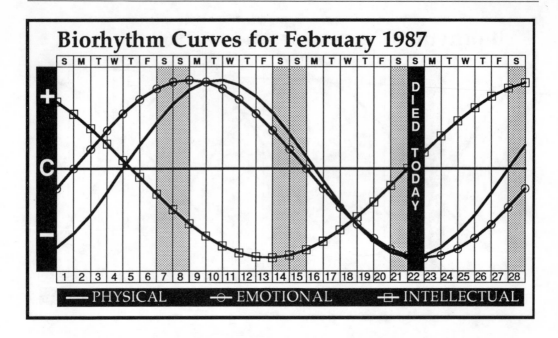

Biorhythm Curves for February 1987

| S M T W T F S | S M T W T F S | S M T W T F S | S M T W T F S |

DIED TODAY

1 2 3 4 5 6 7 8 9 10 11 12 13 14 15 16 17 18 19 20 21 22 23 24 25 26 27 28

—— PHYSICAL   —○— EMOTIONAL   —⊟— INTELLECTUAL

ANDY WARHOL

**d.o.b.
6 August
1928**

The hospital that operated on Andy Warhol on 22 February 1987 either did not know or could not use the biorhythm condition that he was experiencing before going to surgery. Hospitals and clinics that have access to biorhythm information use it to schedule all of their routine operations and, in more pressing cases, use it where possible. The intellectual critical and deep negatives in the other two cycles did not make this an ideal day to operate, in fact the organisations that implement biorhythm avoid critical days for surgery unless of course it is a matter of life and death. If it was a scheduled operation a better time would have been around 10 February when his power of recovery and will to survive would have been at their best.

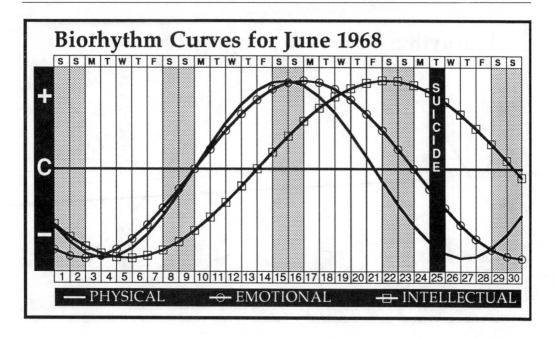

Biorhythm Curves for June 1968

—— PHYSICAL   —○— EMOTIONAL   —□— INTELLECTUAL

The late great British comedian who enthralled millions of television and radio devotees with his ultra successful *Hancock's Half Hour* radio programme, which later transferred equally successfully to television with his unique blend of cynical yet down to earth banter, also had a darker side. Hancock suffered from severe bouts of depression and would often be regarded as moody even by those closest to him. Hancock chose to leave the business for a quieter existence in Australia but ultimately his own 'double life' became the subject of self-scrutiny in the typical Hancock manner. On 24 June 1968 Hancock was passing through an emotionally critical day which saw him descend into one of his deepest depressions so far. The next day, whilst still both emotionally and physically negative, coupled with a strong intellectual positive, Tony Hancock took his own life leaving the simple but clear message ' . . . Life isn't funny anymore'.

TONY HANCOCK

**d.o.b.
12 May
1924**

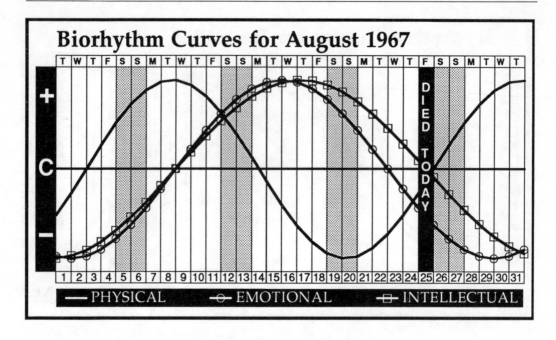

Biorhythm Curves for August 1967

—— PHYSICAL   —⊖— EMOTIONAL   —⊟— INTELLECTUAL

BRIAN EPSTEIN

**d.o.b.
19 September
1934**

The man who discovered the Beatles became their manager and took them to their first major recording contract with EMI. This is the popular image of the likeable English gentleman, but this success was not without cost. By 1967 the Beatles were fully established at the top of their profession, which gave Epstein more time to catch up on the last five years of his life and take stock for the future. A quiet and private man, he had decided to spend a summer weekend at his country home. He set off as scheduled on the morning of Friday 25 August, but almost immediately after arriving he inexplicably turned around the car and returned to his London residence. Epstein's biorhythm condition that day included an intellectual critical which often leads to confused or erratic behaviour. Back home, he locked himself away in his quarters and at some point in the night as his condition was changing to include a physical critical Brian Epstein took his own life.

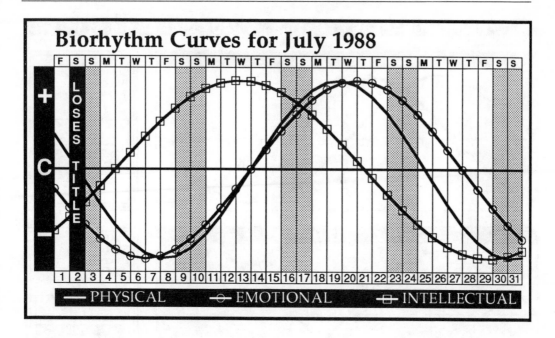

Biorhythm Curves for July 1988

F S S M T W T F S S M T W T F S S M T W T F S S M T W T F S S

+ LOSES TITLE

C

−

1 2 3 4 5 6 7 8 9 10 11 12 13 14 15 16 17 18 19 20 21 22 23 24 25 26 27 28 29 30 31

— PHYSICAL   —⊙— EMOTIONAL   —⊟— INTELLECTUAL

Martina Navratilova was, without doubt, the best woman tennis player of the 1980s and continues to be a major force in the 1990s.

Her record at the Wimbledon championships is still unbeaten, but her winning streak was temporarily broken when she met a West German youngster by the name of Steffi Graf in the final of the 1988 tournament. Martina had won the championship for the past six years and the run looked set to continue until that Saturday afternoon. Her biorhythm condition for the match was far from ideal with a physical critical, and negatives being present in the other two cycles. During the game Martina put up a strong fight in the first set winning it 7-5, but as she weakened Miss Graf simply overpowered her 6-2, 6-1 in the remaining sets to take the title. Martina returned to winning form in 1990 to reverse the result.

**MARTINA
NAVRATILOVA**

**d.o.b.
18 October
1956**

PRINCE CHARLES (14-11-48) & LADY DIANA (1-6-61)

PHYSICAL

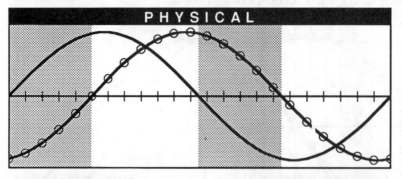

PHYSICAL
Shared Days
Percentage

57%

EXCELLENT
BIORHYTHMIC
COMPATIBILITY

GOOD
BIORHYTHMIC
COMPATIBILITY

LIMITED
BIORHYTHMIC
COMPATIBILITY

EMOTIONAL

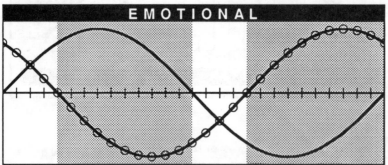

EMOTIONAL
Shared Days
Percentage

29%

EXCELLENT
BIORHYTHMIC
COMPATIBILITY

GOOD
BIORHYTHMIC
COMPATIBILITY

LIMITED
BIORHYTHMIC
COMPATIBILITY

INTELLECTUAL

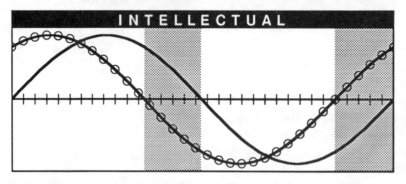

INTELLECTUAL
Shared Days
Percentage

70%

EXCELLENT
BIORHYTHMIC
COMPATIBILITY

GOOD
BIORHYTHMIC
COMPATIBILITY

LIMITED
BIORHYTHMIC
COMPATIBILITY

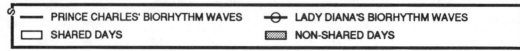

PRINCE CHARLES' BIORHYTHM WAVES   LADY DIANA'S BIORHYTHM WAVES

SHARED DAYS   NON-SHARED DAYS

	PHYSICAL	EMOTIONAL	INTELLECTUAL
Shared Days	13 OUT OF 23	8 OUT OF 28	23 OUT OF 33
Shared Day Percentage	57%	29%	70%
OPTIMUM Number of SHARED Days	23	14	25
Number of Days from Optimum	10	6	2
COMPATIBILITY Percentage	57%	57%	92%

OVERALL COMPATIBILITY PERCENTAGE

69%

EXCELLENT

Overall Biorhythmic

Compatibility

The marriage in 1982 between the heir to the throne and the shy lady with the film star looks was often portrayed as a marriage made in heaven. Indeed, this statement would seem to hold true even after detailed biorhythmic analysis, despite occasional reports to the contrary. Their physical and emotional compatibility of 57 per cent provides a good basic harmony between the two parties. For most of the time they will share a similar level of energy and drive, and their ability and desire to help each other in times of emotional stress will be strong. The relationship should not be prone to becoming stale as there are plenty of days when the couple do not share similar conditions. The excellent intellectual figure of 92 per cent means that Charles and Diana will be 'on the same plane' for most of the time, and still have a few days when their conditions will differ enough to enable one partner to back up the other. With an overall compatibility figure of 69 per cent it is fair to say that the forecast for their future success and happiness is excellent. In summary, they have enough similarity in daily conditions to make a close and loving relationship, whilst still having enough differences to keep them on their toes.

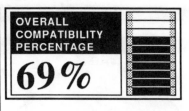

PRINCE CHARLES AND PRINCESS DIANA

WOODY ALLEN (1-12-35) & MIA FARROW (9-2-45)

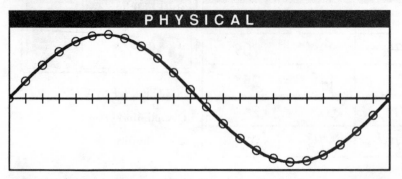

PHYSICAL
Shared Days
Percentage
100%
EXCELLENT
BIORHYTHMIC
COMPATIBILITY

GOOD
BIORHYTHMIC
COMPATIBILITY

LIMITED
BIORHYTHMIC
COMPATIBILITY

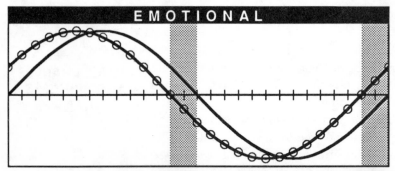

EMOTIONAL
Shared Days
Percentage
86%
EXCELLENT
BIORHYTHMIC
COMPATIBILITY

GOOD
BIORHYTHMIC
COMPATIBILITY

LIMITED
BIORHYTHMIC
COMPATIBILITY

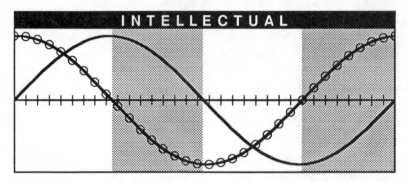

INTELLECTUAL
Shared Days
Percentage
52%
EXCELLENT
BIORHYTHMIC
COMPATIBILITY

GOOD
BIORHYTHMIC
COMPATIBILITY

LIMITED
BIORHYTHMIC
COMPATIBILITY

—— WOODY'S BIORHYTHM WAVES	—⊖— MIA'S BIORHYTHM WAVES
☐ SHARED DAYS	▨ NON-SHARED DAYS

	PHYSICAL	EMOTIONAL	INTELLECTUAL
Shared Days	23 OUT OF 23	24 OUT OF 28	17 OUT OF 33
Shared Day Percentage	100%	86%	52%
OPTIMUM Number of SHARED Days	23	14	25
Number of Days from Optimum	0	10	8
COMPATIBILITY Percentage	100%	29%	68%

OVERALL COMPATIBILITY PERCENTAGE

66%

EXCELLENT

Overall Biorhythmic

Compatibility

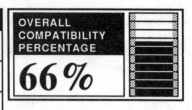

WOODY ALLEN AND MIA FARROW

Both Woody Allen and Mia Farrow had been involved in more than one unsuccessful partnership before they 'met over a movie' and began what has become, in their own words, the perfect relationship. Biorhythm certainly wouldn't argue with that, as the bedrock of any union between two people is their physical compatibility, and with a 100 per cent rating you can't do much better than that! They are naturally suited to each other and should not suffer from potentially damaging physical conflicts which can arise. However, it is as well that they have such a strong foundation to build upon as their emotional compatibility is limited, and this part of their relationship will be characterised by very hot and very cool times. This is due to the very high number of days when they will have the same condition, which means that one week they will both be on a high whilst the next they could both be on a low. The intellectual compatibility rating of 68 per cent should ensure that any joint projects will have balanced input from both sides with just about the right amount of difference to ensure that there is often scope for debate. An overall rating of 66 per cent is excellent and should see this relationship generating a lot of happiness and understanding.

ROBERT WAGNER (10-2-30) & NATALIE WOOD (20-7-38)

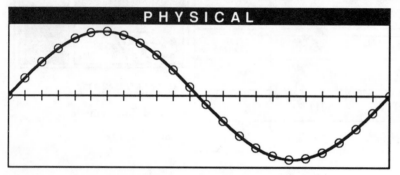

PHYSICAL
Shared Days
Percentage
100%

EXCELLENT
BIORHYTHMIC
COMPATIBILITY

GOOD
BIORHYTHMIC
COMPATIBILITY

LIMITED
BIORHYTHMIC
COMPATIBILITY

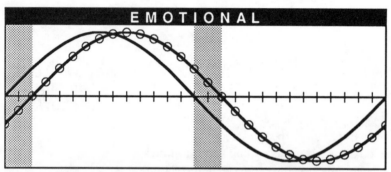

EMOTIONAL
Shared Days
Percentage
86%

EXCELLENT
BIORHYTHMIC
COMPATIBILITY

GOOD
BIORHYTHMIC
COMPATIBILITY

LIMITED
BIORHYTHMIC
COMPATIBILITY

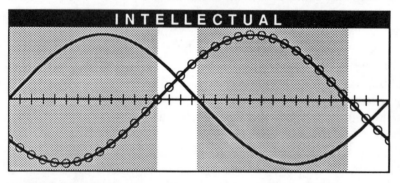

INTELLECTUAL
Shared Days
Percentage
21%

EXCELLENT
BIORHYTHMIC
COMPATIBILITY

GOOD
BIORHYTHMIC
COMPATIBILITY

LIMITED
BIORHYTHMIC
COMPATIBILITY

—— **ROBERT'S BIORHYTHM WAVES**   —⊖— **NATALIE'S BIORHYTHM WAVES**

▭ **SHARED DAYS**   ▨ **NON-SHARED DAYS**

	PHYSICAL	EMOTIONAL	INTELLECTUAL
Shared Days	23 OUT OF 23	24 OUT OF 28	7 OUT OF 33
Shared Day Percentage	100%	86%	21%
OPTIMUM Number of SHARED Days	23	14	25
Number of Days from Optimum	0	10	18
COMPATIBILITY Percentage	100%	29%	28%

OVERALL COMPATIBILITY PERCENTAGE

52%

GOOD

Overall Biorhythmic Compatibility

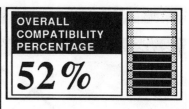
ROBERT WAGNER AND NATALIE WOOD

This case history is especially interesting from the viewpoint that the couple married, went through the pain of a divorce, only to decide to remarry some years later! Between Wagner and Wood there was a good overall compatibility of 52 per cent which in itself does not give us any clue as to why this should occur. However, a deeper look into the individual biorhythm cycles reveals a very interesting set of ratings, namely that whilst they were 100 per cent physically compatible, with all the positive influences this can bring to bear, they were only 28 per cent intellectually compatible. Once again the very high physical rating brings with it an almost irresistible force of attraction between two people spending any length of time together, but if a truly happy and long lasting relationship is to be achieved then this must be balanced by good ratings in the remaining cycles. It is difficult to hypothesise, but it would seem logical to suggest that, despite the extremely high initial attraction, it was not possible to sustain it for any length of time due to the other biorhythmic factors conspiring against them. Once separated, however, they would have found it difficult to experience such a high physical compatibilty with another partner.

ERNIE WISE (27-11-25) & ERIC MORECAMBE (14-5-26)

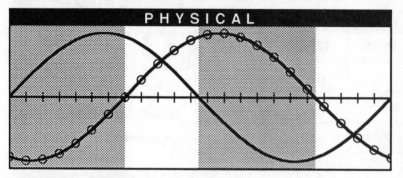

P H Y S I C A L

PHYSICAL
Shared Days
Percentage
39%

EXCELLENT
BIORHYTHMIC
COMPATIBILITY

GOOD
BIORHYTHMIC
COMPATIBILITY

LIMITED
BIORHYTHMIC
COMPATIBILITY

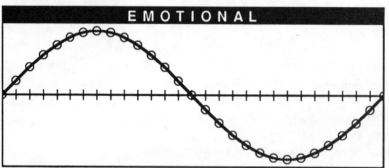

E M O T I O N A L

EMOTIONAL
Shared Days
Percentage
100%

EXCELLENT
BIORHYTHMIC
COMPATIBILITY

GOOD
BIORHYTHMIC
COMPATIBILITY

LIMITED
BIORHYTHMIC
COMPATIBILITY

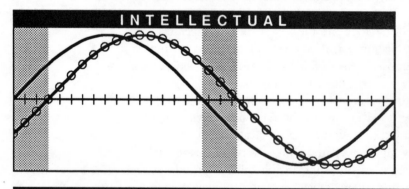

I N T E L L E C T U A L

INTELLECTUAL
Shared Days
Percentage
82%

EXCELLENT
BIORHYTHMIC
COMPATIBILITY

GOOD
BIORHYTHMIC
COMPATIBILITY

LIMITED
BIORHYTHMIC
COMPATIBILITY

— ERNIE'S BIORHYTHM WAVES   ⊖ ERIC'S BIORHYTHM WAVES

☐ SHARED DAYS   ▒ NON-SHARED DAYS

	PHYSICAL	EMOTIONAL	INTELLECTUAL
Shared Days	9 OUT OF 23	28 OUT OF 28	27 OUT OF 33
Shared Day Percentage	39%	100%	82%
OPTIMUM Number of SHARED Days	23	14	25
Number of Days from Optimum	14	14	2
COMPATIBILITY Percentage	39%	0%	92%

OVERALL COMPATIBILITY PERCENTAGE

44%

GOOD

Overall Biorhythmic

Compatibility

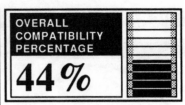

ERIC MORECAMBE AND ERNIE WISE

Morecambe and Wise illustrate an interesting example of a business partnership that worked to perfection with the public. The unique type of humour and comedy that these two delivered on stage was a hit with millions of people all over the world in the 1970s and most of the 1980s until the untimely death of Eric Morecambe. The fact that they worked well as a team is not really surprising when you consider how close their emotional and intellectual cycles are to each other. In a normal sexual relationship this level of emotional compatibility is not ideal, but in this particular type of partnership it is almost an advantage. Emotionally and intellectually they were almost always in the same condition and it could be said that one never really outshone the other; they simply worked perfectly with each other. Their physical compatibility rating of 39 caused no problems for their particular type of partnership.

RICHARD BURTON (10-11-25) & ELIZABETH TAYLOR (27-2-32)

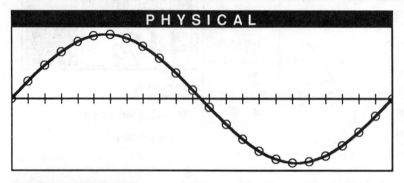

PHYSICAL
Shared Days
Percentage
100%

| EXCELLENT BIORHYTHMIC COMPATIBILITY |
| GOOD BIORHYTHMIC COMPATIBILITY |
| LIMITED BIORHYTHMIC COMPATIBILITY |

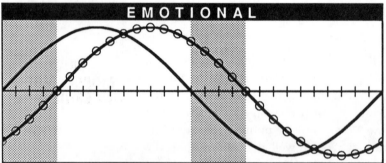

EMOTIONAL
Shared Days
Percentage
71%

| EXCELLENT BIORHYTHMIC COMPATIBILITY |
| GOOD BIORHYTHMIC COMPATIBILITY |
| LIMITED BIORHYTHMIC COMPATIBILITY |

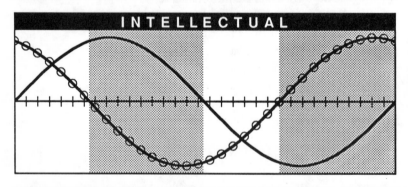

INTELLECTUAL
Shared Days
Percentage
39%

| EXCELLENT BIORHYTHMIC COMPATIBILITY |
| GOOD BIORHYTHMIC COMPATIBILITY |
| LIMITED BIORHYTHMIC COMPATIBILITY |

--- RICHARD'S BIORHYTHM WAVES　　　　-O- ELIZABETH'S BIORHYTHM WAVES

☐ SHARED DAYS　　　　▨ NON-SHARED DAYS

	PHYSICAL	EMOTIONAL	INTELLECTUAL
Shared Days	23 OUT OF 23	20 OUT OF 28	13 OUT OF 33
Shared Day Percentage	100%	71%	39%
OPTIMUM Number of SHARED Days	23	14	25
Number of Days from Optimum	0	6	12
COMPATIBILITY Percentage	100%	57%	52%

OVERALL COMPATIBILITY PERCENTAGE

70%

EXCELLENT

Overall Biorhythmic

Compatibility

ELIZABETH TAYLOR AND RICHARD BURTON

Probably the most talked about, written about and filmed on/off relationship of all time. Burton and Taylor married twice, divorced twice and, according to many observers, almost married again for the third time. Why? Well, this couple had a 100 per cent rating in their physical compatibility which is not an everyday occurence, as the statistical likelihood of this is only 1 in 23. Their overall biorhythm rating of 70 per cent is very high and should really have made for an ideal relationship. However, in this case you have to look closely at the people involved and their personal situations. Both of them were constantly in the public eye and a degree of competition could well have existed between them. Situations like this have traditionally put an overpowering amount of strain on ideal relationships and in the world of show business the pressures that exist are far stronger than in a normal relationship. Their high ratings would have made a strong bond between them, which is probably the reason for their second trip down the aisle and for the fact that they remained friends up until Burton's death in 1984.

ROD STEWART (1-10-45) & RACHEL HUNTER (8-9-68)

PHYSICAL

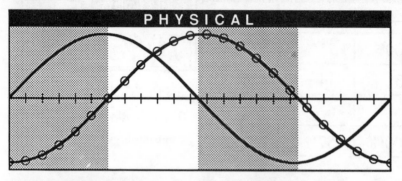

PHYSICAL
Shared Days
Percentage
48%

EXCELLENT
BIORHYTHMIC
COMPATIBILITY

GOOD
BIORHYTHMIC
COMPATIBILITY

LIMITED
BIORHYTHMIC
COMPATIBILITY

EMOTIONAL

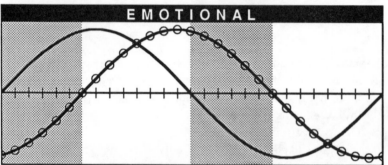

EMOTIONAL
Shared Days
Percentage
57%

EXCELLENT
BIORHYTHMIC
COMPATIBILITY

GOOD
BIORHYTHMIC
COMPATIBILITY

LIMITED
BIORHYTHMIC
COMPATIBILITY

INTELLECTUAL

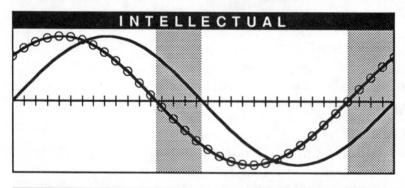

INTELLECTUAL
Shared Days
Percentage
76%

EXCELLENT
BIORHYTHMIC
COMPATIBILITY

GOOD
BIORHYTHMIC
COMPATIBILITY

LIMITED
BIORHYTHMIC
COMPATIBILITY

—— ROD'S BIORHYTHM WAVES   —O— RACHEL'S BIORHYTHM WAVES

☐ SHARED DAYS   ▦ NON-SHARED DAYS

	PHYSICAL	EMOTIONAL	INTELLECTUAL
Shared Days	11 OUT OF 23	16 OUT OF 28	25 OUT OF 33
Shared Day Percentage	48%	.57%	76%
OPTIMUM Number of SHARED Days	23	14	25
Number of Days from Optimum	12	2	0
COMPATIBILITY Percentage	48%	86%	100%

OVERALL COMPATIBILITY PERCENTAGE

78%

EXCELLENT

Overall Biorhythmic

Compatibility

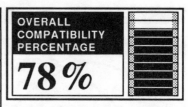

ROD STEWART AND RACHEL HUNTER

The marriage between this couple was the result of a real whirlwind romance and this is well reflected in their overall biorhythm compatibility of 78 per cent. Their good physical rating of 48 per cent should see them reasonably balanced in all matters of a physical nature. When this figure is combined with a very high emotional rating of 86 per cent it would appear that the prospects for the future are getting better all of the time. There will be an even spread of those times when common projects are best tackled jointly and those times when Rachel's 'highs' will be able to sustain Rod during his low periods, and vice versa. With an intellectual compatibility rating of 100 per cent there should never be a time when one partner is consistently outperforming the other in matters of thought and reasoning, and this should be a particularly balanced relationship with both parties receiving much from and, just as importantly, giving much to the other. Maybe Rachel is the woman who will finally be able to hold onto one of rock's greats.

BING CROSBY (3-5-03) & BOB HOPE (29-5-03)

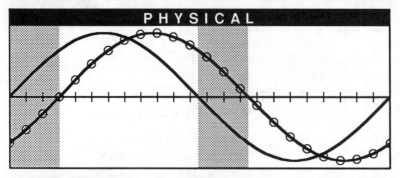

PHYSICAL

PHYSICAL
Shared Days
Percentage
74%

EXCELLENT
BIORHYTHMIC
COMPATIBILITY

GOOD
BIORHYTHMIC
COMPATIBILITY

LIMITED
BIORHYTHMIC
COMPATIBILITY

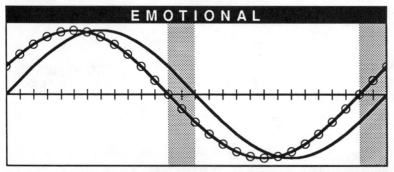

EMOTIONAL

EMOTIONAL
Shared Days
Percentage
86%

EXCELLENT
BIORHYTHMIC
COMPATIBILITY

GOOD
BIORHYTHMIC
COMPATIBILITY

LIMITED
BIORHYTHMIC
COMPATIBILITY

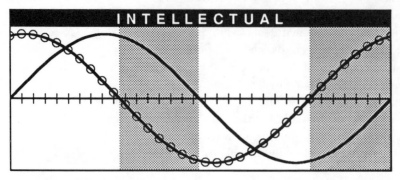

INTELLECTUAL

INTELLECTUAL
Shared Days
Percentage
58%

EXCELLENT
BIORHYTHMIC
COMPATIBILITY

GOOD
BIORHYTHMIC
COMPATIBILITY

LIMITED
BIORHYTHMIC
COMPATIBILITY

— BING'S BIORHYTHM WAVES   —O— BOB'S BIORHYTHM WAVES

☐ SHARED DAYS   ▨ NON-SHARED DAYS

	PHYSICAL	EMOTIONAL	INTELLECTUAL
Shared Days	17 OUT OF 23	24 OUT OF 28	19 OUT OF 33
Shared Day Percentage	74%	86%	58%
OPTIMUM Number of SHARED Days	23	14	25
Number of Days from Optimum	6	10	6
COMPATIBILITY Percentage	74%	29%	76%

OVERALL COMPATIBILITY PERCENTAGE

60%

GOOD

Overall Biorhythmic

Compatibility

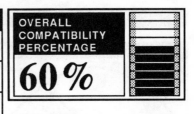

BING CROSBY AND BOB HOPE

The favourite comedy duo made famous during the *Road to . . .* series of films produced during the 1940s was, in many ways, well suited to the demanding task of producing and sustaining two of the most famous 'made for film' characters. For a start, the series was a physically demanding prospect and their excellent rating of 74 per cent was well placed to ensure that neither party was either lagging too far behind or pushing too far ahead in physical matters. When turning out several films a year this factor is not to be underestimated. Secondly, within film circles, this pair was infamous (to the horror of many a script writer) for ad-libbing lines in front of the camera during the live recordings. This ad-libbing became more and more a part of the routine which is understandable when one looks at their intellectual compatibility of 76 per cent and their emotional shared day rating of 86 per cent. This would have allowed one of them, as they would both normally be in the same condition, to follow his own script without fear that he was leaving his partner out on a literal limb. An often copied but seldom successful routine that to this biorhythmically matched couple was almost like falling off a log!

STAN LAUREL (16-6-1890) & OLIVER HARDY (18-1-1892)

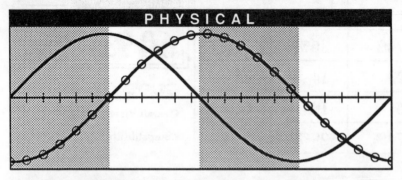

P H Y S I C A L

PHYSICAL
Shared Days
Percentage
48%

EXCELLENT
BIORHYTHMIC
COMPATIBILITY

GOOD
BIORHYTHMIC
COMPATIBILITY

LIMITED
BIORHYTHMIC
COMPATIBILITY

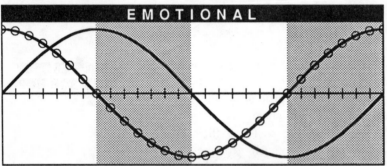

E M O T I O N A L

EMOTIONAL
Shared Days
Percentage
50%

EXCELLENT
BIORHYTHMIC
COMPATIBILITY

GOOD
BIORHYTHMIC
COMPATIBILITY

LIMITED
BIORHYTHMIC
COMPATIBILITY

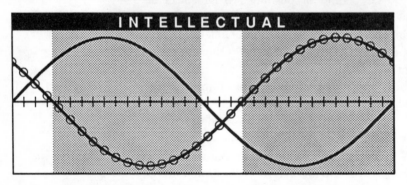

I N T E L L E C T U A L

INTELLECTUAL
Shared Days
Percentage
21%

EXCELLENT
BIORHYTHMIC
COMPATIBILITY

GOOD
BIORHYTHMIC
COMPATIBILITY

LIMITED
BIORHYTHMIC
COMPATIBILITY

 STAN'S BIORHYTHM WAVES    OLIVER'S BIORHYTHM WAVES

SHARED DAYS   NON-SHARED DAYS

	PHYSICAL	EMOTIONAL	INTELLECTUAL
Shared Days	11 OUT OF 23	14 OUT OF 28	7 OUT OF 33
Shared Day Percentage	48%	50%	21%
OPTIMUM Number of SHARED Days	23	14	25
Number of Days from Optimum	12	0	18
COMPATIBILITY Percentage	48%	100%	28%

OVERALL COMPATIBILITY PERCENTAGE

59%

GOOD

Overall Biorhythmic

Compatibility

STAN LAUREL AND OLIVER HARDY

This was one of the most famous and certainly one of the first and funniest screen slapstick double acts that the world has witnessed. Laurel and Hardy were portrayed as the bumbling pair who remained together through thick and thin. The most significant aspect of their biorhythm compatibility is their 100 per cent emotional compatibility rating which is well reflected in how they felt about each other off-screen. Laurel and Hardy were the closest of friends and their relationship stood the test of time. They made over 200 films, mainly in the 1920s and 1930s, and performed in the Royal Variety Show at the London Palladium in 1947. Oliver Hardy died in 1957 and Stan Laurel was deeply affected by his death because, as he put it, they were 'like brothers'.

Their overall rating of 59 per cent is very suitable for a team such as this and holds a good balance for most of the activities involved in their work. Hardy was never to find in matrimony the security he enjoyed with Laurel in their close friendship and was married four times. As an outstanding partnership, they will never be forgotten and their work remains popular to this day.

USING BIORHYTHM

The use and interpretation of biorhythm is generally considered to be both a subjective business and a question of personal taste and understanding. It is necessary at this point to reinforce the correct usages and how they relate to the user. People may comment on their biorhythm with relation to, say, an aeroplane trip in the context of 'I'm triple minus today, I have a bad feeling about this flight.' Of course biorhythm will effect how you deal with the flight and how good you feel at the other end, but to relate your biorhythm condition to the possibility of an air disaster is nonsense. The actual possibility of an air disaster is dependent on the people responsible for the flight such as the pilot and air traffic controllers and their particular biorhythmic conditions. To some this may sound obvious, but it is surprising how many people fall at this fundamental hurdle and fail to see the true benefits of biorhythmic study. This also happens when couples compare their biorhythm compatibilities with such gems as 'I knew we would have good physical compatibility because he has a nice body'. Again, this demonstrates a singular lack of understanding of biorhythm compatibility and what it is saying. Before one can actually use biorhythm effectively one should understand that it relates to specific aspects of everyday life and does not attempt to be a mathematical crystal ball. If you want your fortune told in specific terms then biorhythm is not the way to go about it. What biorhythm is, is a method of seeing what shape you will be in to deal with everyday and not-so-everyday events.

Biorhythm can be described as a potential of your ability. If you view the three waves as 'energy' levels and read them as such you would be close to the real meaning of the science. The critical axis (the mathematical zero) represents your average of potential in each of the three waves. Obviously, as one gets older this average will change. For example, if we look at the physical cycle, the average of a 20-year old man's physical capacity will be better than that of a 50-year old. The point here is that biorhythm is not an absolute but a relative reading; relative to the individual in question. The ups and downs expressed in the biorhythm cycles are how you relate to this average, and this is one of the most important considerations when reading a biorhythm chart. You must remember that it is a personal science that deals with both your average capacity and how the forecast for the day in question relates to that capacity.

When studying your own biorhythm positions it is for you to choose the amount of detail you wish to extract from them. In some cases you may be satisfied with knowing that you are in a particular phase, say positive or negative, but there are times when it will be worth looking further into each of the conditions to see exactly what stage of the cycle you are in. The patterns of the three cycles are similar in their basic sinusoidal curve form, and for all three conditions within them (positive, negative and critical) they will be either on a rising or falling part of the cycle. This is significant in many cases as it would seem logical, for example, that a positive physical cycle condition on a particular day would have more effect if it happened to be on an upswing rather than after the peak of the cycle. This aspect of biorhythm can be applied to all three cycles and is influenced by what is commonly termed the 'mini-critical'. The mini-critical is the point during a cycle where the direction of the curve changes from either upwards to downwards or vice versa. The effect of this particular occurrence is not as pronounced as the full blown critical day but can be noticed in certain circumstances and does need to be understood.

The mini-critical represents the centre of either the peak or the trough in any of the cycles. This aspect of the biorhythm cycles will break down each of the phases into a further division that can be useful for getting to know the more subtle influences of biorhythm. Taking account of the mini-critical that exists will show you in what direction you are moving in each of the cycles and will indicate whether you are on a decline or increase in the strength in each of your cycles.

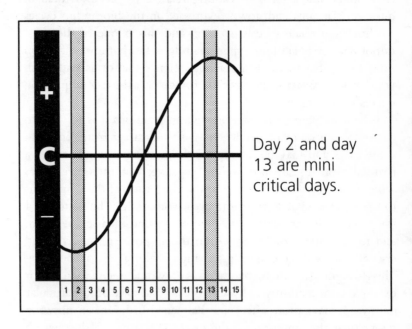

Day 2 and day 13 are mini critical days.

The Mini Critical Day

By now you should have a comprehensive understanding of the rules and laws that make up biorhythm and so the next step of actually applying the science to your own life should be a relatively straightforward one. You will know better than anyone which particular aspects of your life need improvement, or indeed any areas where you think that biorhythm may be able to offer you information that has previously been unavailable to you.

The biorhythm calculator in this book can be used on a month-by-month basis or alternatively you could set up the chart for each month of the year and photocopy it so that you have your biorhythm information for the whole year at hand. By doing this you can then glance ahead to look at your biorhythm positions for events that will be taking place in the future, giving you a very good forward planning guide.

When you begin to apply biorhythm in your life it is important to give yourself a chance to tune in to the science because, as discussed earlier, the effects of the science will vary from person to person. Everybody has very different levels of association with biorhythm and the level to which you are affected will become evident only after a period of application.

THE BLIND DIARY

Before you venture into applied biorhythm you can use a well tried and tested method that will almost certainly offer you a relatively quick and accurate way to determine how affected you are by the changing cycle positions. The Blind Diary will help you obtain an unbiased view of the way you correlate to the prevailing biorhythm conditions at the time.

The best way to apply this technique is to monitor the way you feel and perform during a pre-set period while you are unaware of your biorhythm conditions. The 'unaware' factor is of paramount importance, and will help you to see which aspects of your daily performance and behaviour seem to be most affected by biorhythm. It is important to let this exercise run over a significant period in order to experience a cross section of different situations. If you follow a Blind Diary process for a month then you will come into contact with many of the biorhythm conditions that exist. However, certain combinations, such as double criticals, will not always be present during this period as they only occur about four or five times a year, although you should, on the whole, encounter a sufficiently varied set of conditions within this period to offer you a fairly accurate ongoing guide.

If you find that this process does not correlate to your biorhythm chart then it is possible that the circumstances or the situations in which you find yourself are not challenging enough actually to enable the effects of biorhythm to be felt sufficiently.

Noticing The Changes

Everything in life, including the functions of the body, are far from regular but we tend to not notice these subtle changes. Activities such as shaving in the morning can, if studied closely, reveal that the skin is affected by some kind of cycle. If you think about it you will realise that there are days when the skin is very sensitive, resulting in easy cuts or rashes, and other days where you could drag a rusty blade across your skin without so much as a blemish appearing. Another heavily researched area is the sex drive which been found to vary over periods of time. Consider also your general moods and intellectual sharpness, your ability for coordination, your general vitality – all these things are subject to changes, some regular as clockwork, others not so. Only when you are able to distil these aspects of your own behaviour will you be able to apply biorhythm and get the results that will change your life. It is important to understand that not all of your bodily functions will seem to be influenced by biorhythm, but you need to consider all the different variables to get an accurate overall picture.

Biorhythm does not have to be used as a tool to alter these differences in our make up but it is surely an advantage to have this closer understanding of the body and the way that its performance will be subject to subtle changes. Much of the biorhythm theory may seem to defy logical explanation, which has in the past been a stumbling block for its acceptance, and it is only right to be sceptical about something until it has been proved to you. The Blind Diary laid out on the following pages for your use has a number of suggested areas that you should monitor but feel free to choose any areas that you think will be

of most interest to you. If you don't wish to write in this book
then copy the page or design your own format.

THE BLIND DIARY

Use the P, E and I boxes to rate the way you feel and perform using 10 as the best score.
Use the rest of the table to make any notes that you feel are applicable.

DAY No.	P	E	I	NOTES
1				
2				
3				
4				
5				
6				
7				
8				
9				
10				
11				
12				
13				

DAY No.	P	E	I	NOTES
14				
15				
16				
17				
18				
19				
20				
21				
22				
23				
24				
25				
26				
27				
28				
29				
30				

Once you have carried out the Blind Diary exercise you should be able to make direct comparisons between the two sets of results. Areas where a direct correlation takes place can then be used to help you compensate for or even enhance certain parts of your behaviour and performance. You may find that during a physical and emotional high you are full of energy and vitality, so this is the time really to go for it with activities that push you physically, as the benefits to be gained during this period will never be bettered. At the other end of the scale, during times when there is a direct link between bouts of depression or temper flares and your prevailing biorhythm condition, you should use this information to pre-warn yourself that you will not be at your best in these areas and a certain level of compensatory action may be required.

The exercise should not be taken as absolute because for the data to be considered totally accurate it would be safer to run the blind diary procedure a number of times, but as a guide to determining your basic level of correlation to biorhythm it is more than adequate.

Reacting To The Results

Once you are armed with your biorhythm information and you have established the areas that affect you it will become an easy and satisfying exercise fully to apply the science to yourself. Using biorhythm as a daily guide to your expected level of performance is something that should be encouraged, as one will almost always come across unplanned situations for which one would benefit from being biorhythmically prepared. It is important to learn to use the science to a degree that sees you constantly aware of your weaknesses and strengths in the three cycles, and this will become automatic when you refer to your chart on a regular basis.

Of the many activities for which we regularly plan ahead, such as decorating the house or servicing the car, biorhythm can easily be applied to maximise not only the final success of the project

GETTING THE BEST OUT OF YOURSELF

but also the enjoyment of carrying out the exercise itself. When you plan to get involved in any activity, reference to your biorhythm condition should enable you to get the best result. If, for example, you decide to redecorate your home, it would be wise carefully to consider your biorhythm condition. If you find yourself in an emotionally high position you will no doubt have a lot of enthusiasm and creative flair to tackle the task, but it should be noted that this type of condition could actually see you going a little over the top. It is important to approach this type of activity with a balanced head, because periods of emotional highs, while being a great time to get stuck in, often need to be tempered with rational thought. If this type of approach is employed, then the results should come out in the desired way. There is, of course, nothing to stop you using your emotional highs to generate new ideas and concepts relating to the interior design that you want to achieve, but it is sensible to reflect on these ideas a few days later once your biorhythm conditions have entered a more predictable phase.

Kicking The Habit

Biorhythm can be used to help in a number of areas that have traditionally been extremely hard to get to grips with, like dieting, giving up smoking, taking regular exercise, and any other activity that requires high levels of willpower and commitment. The application of biorhythm here requires a little thought and planning but if employed correctly it has a good chance of success as, after all, success in these areas is almost always down to the state of mind of the individual concerned. So, how does a smoker go about using biorhythm to help overcome the habit? Like most of the resolutions that we make the timing of them is always significant. The traditional time is in the New Year as this is usually associated with a fresh start. To time these attempts to best suit your biorhythm conditions you have to look at more than just the position of one particular cycle as all three have a part to play.

Also you should establish when the effort of your intended good deed is going to begin really to bite into your willpower and good intentions. For example, it is not advisable to start a no-smoking campaign when your biorhythm position is at the best position to offer you increased resolve, as that should occur when the desire for a cigarette is at its highest – about four or five days after giving up. In order to increase the chance of success it would be useful to eliminate as many pressure situations during the hardest part of the exercise, as it is usually when we are placed under stress that our resolve will weaken and we find ourselves back where we started. The most important cycles to consider when planning the start date of your attempt are the emotional and intellectual cycles as these will have a strong effect on your mental stability and can, if timed correctly, make the difference between winning or losing the battle.

Anybody who wishes to start a no-smoking campaign or a diet is capable of lasting at least three days if they really set their minds to it so, using the previous example, the position of the emotional and intellectual cycles should be such that after three days they are moving in a positive upward direction. To achieve this you may have to wait a few days to find the ideal position. It is far more important to calculate the most positive biorhythmic conditions at the point where your resolve will best be backed up by the strengths affected by these two categories. You will then have a period of around two emotionally and intellectually positive weeks to help in dealing with the trauma that this activity can cause. After two weeks you should have established a routine in which you can operate without giving in to the craving. The going will stay tough for a few weeks after that but your initial success and the fact that your biorhythm pattern will soon return to periods where willpower will be backed up by strong mental resolve should help you through the most trying times.

Get Fit And Stay Healthy

As biorhythm can reveal so much of a very personal nature it provides an ideal opportunity to put the science to work on the body in a manner that will produce noticeable results and bring long-term benefits. Exercise is vital to health, and as we get older the need to maintain regular exercise is very important if we are to avoid heart disease and weight problems.

Biorhythm can aid a personal exercise programme in a number of ways, showing both good times for activity and times when caution needs to observed. It is important, however, to make sure that we do not take our exercise programmes too far, and cause injury. Taking biorhythm into consideration in this area of activity will offer you two main advantages. The first advantage is awareness of the strengths and weaknesses in your physical position which should help you determine the level to which you should be pushing yourself. Of course, if you are only interested in gentle workouts then you should be able to cope regardless of your physical position. It is, however, more important to be aware of your strengths and weaknesses if you take your exercise seriously and to a higher level. The second advantage of being aware of your biorhythm cycle positions during exercise and sport is to be aware of any potentially dangerous situations that can be caused by the presence of a critical in any one of your three cycles. As we are already aware of the accident-prone nature of critical days, it is advisable to remind yourself that you are open to mistakes and errors of judgement. This point should not be treated lightly because many people have suffered injuries or accidents while exercising or playing sport that have affected them for the rest of their lives. During a critical day a sure-footed step should prevail and you should always give a second thought to situations that require you to push yourself.

For competitive sportspeople biorhythmic awareness of yourself and your opponents can give you an advantage that is equal to hours of practice. To be aware of any limitations to your ability on a particular day can enable you to play the game in the way that is best suited to your disposition. This potential can be witnessed when you watch many one-on-one sports where one or even both of the competitors must change their strategy midway through a game because the results are not as expected. Had these people been pre-warned of their biorhythmic suitability for a particular strategy, they could have started the game with the right approach. You will find with experimentation that it is possible to use strategy instead of brawn on certain days and still put up a performance that you are more than happy with. The importance lies in making the decision before the event so that you can put up a balanced and efficient display. Biorhythm is there to be used; if it is left lying dormant you will certainly miss opportunities to get the maximum out of yourself.

Taking A Holiday

The planning involved in choosing the location, type and time of a holiday is normally considered at length before any decisions are actually taken. This is an area that can also benefit greatly from consideration of your biorhythm positions during the planning stage. If you are taking the holiday with a partner or friend then of course it is advisable also to take their conditions into consideration. As most holidays are a combination of many different types of activity, from sunbathing to sightseeing, right through to energetic walks in the local terrain, there are obviously a number of differing demands placed on the individual. Taking account of your biorhythm position in this context will serve to increase your enjoyment of the holiday. The best way to deal with the planning of activities that you will take part in while you are away is to try, where possible, to plan them around the best phases that are available to you. It is not always possible to choose dates that are best suited to you biorhythmically, but it is possible to get the best out of the time that is available. It is also wise to be aware of the possible critical situations that may be present in your cycles especially if you are going to take part in any slightly risky activities such as water skiing, the dreaded black ski run, or scuba diving.

Using Your Mind

The work carried by Alfred Teltscher in the late 1920s revolved around the effects of the intellectual cycle, and his observations about the varying abilities of the mind can be employed to good effect when it comes to learning new subjects or dealing with problems that are mentally demanding. During the positive phase of the intellectual cycle there is an excellent opportunity to digest new information and the ability to retain the data is excellent. Awareness of the position of your intellectual cycle will help you in many areas that are open to improvement or are constantly used. If you tend to forget something unless you write it down or use some other way to remind yourself to do a particular task, here is an opportunity actually to put your mind's ability to the test. Once you get into the habit of making notes to avoid forgetting something it is usually a trait that will stay with you. This is not always such a bad thing, but we are gifted with a magnificent instrument between our ears and we should learn to use it to its full. So, during the times where your intellectual ability is in a positive phase try and put your powers of recall to the test and you will be surprised with the results. Preoccupation affects the ability to be mentally sharp, so being easily distracted does not aid the task of dealing with demanding mental issues. We all suffer from these lapses in concentration but often they come and go with the same regularity as the intellectual cycle. Once you are in tune with the delicate workings of your mind it becomes far easier to compensate for the periods when your intellectual ability is reduced. It is only in this sector that you should really need to be writing yourself notes and reminders.

We are all looking for ways to improve our lives and operate more efficiently and the mind plays a vital role in achieving our goals. If we can't rely on ourselves to make the most of opportunities that present themselves then it is likely that we will fall short of the mark in the achievement of our aims. Use the positive aspects of the intellectual cycle to re-educate your ability to learn and digest new areas of information. There is a saying, 'anything is possible if you put your mind to it', and this is very appropriate when considered in the context of the intellectual cycle.

Biorhythm can play a very revealing role within relationships and the question of compatibility is often very significant in determining whether a relationship will be successful. In Chapter 3 the calculations required to work out your compatibility are shown, but there is a lot more to be said about how to deal with your relevant biorhythmic compatibility.

BIORHTHM FOR TWO

To get a visual view of how you match up to your partner or anybody else with whom you wish to compare your biorhythm, you should use the calculator in this book to set up each of your biorhythm conditions for the same month in the same year. As there is only one calculator in this book you will really need to make a copy of one of the charts so that you can effectively run a side by side comparison. When this comparison is made it should become clear to you how your biorhythm conditions visually compare. It is important to remember that your compared conditions will always remain constant, for example, if you can see that your physical cycle starts anew on the 7th and your partner's starts on the 11th, then this four-day gap will always remain the same. The same will, of course, apply to the relevant positions in each of your other cycles. If you have an up-to-date biorhythm chart you will always be able to tell where your partner's biorhythm positions are simply by relating them to each of your cycles. If your partner is diametrically opposed to you in the emotional cycle then whenever you are at your peak they will be at their lowest point and vice versa. Not only that, but you will always share the same critical days!

In terms of getting the best out of a relationship the information that you can draw on from this compatibility exercise can help to reduce any stress or differences that may exist, or heighten certain activities. This is best achieved by looking for periods that are not well suited between you and by compensating for them with the understanding that biorhythm knowledge can bring. For example, the above-mentioned emotional cycle positions could be potentially explosive because of the opposite influences that each will have and the fact that both partners share critical days. However, this information should help to avoid confrontations and lead to a deeper and more relaxed understanding of the situation.

While it is preferable to have a good degree of overall compatibility there is no reason why two people can't get on well and stay together without it, providing that there is a good level of understanding in the relationship, the understanding that awareness of each other's biorhythm positions can bring.

When looking at respective biorhythm positions you should try to look at ideal times to take part in joint activities of all forms. It is also interesting to try a number of different activities at differing times during your cycles to see if there are any times that are really well suited, a kind of mutual blind diary if you like. Sex drive and sexual harmony can be linked into biorhythm through the physical and emotional cycles and it has been found that there are certain periods within a couple's compatibility that are far better suited to one partner than the other, so it is important to find mutual periods in your cycles.

In a fiery relationship, which still manages to stand the test of time, there is a real opportunity to let biorhythm smooth out the differences. This is because the countless and petty arguments that take place are often attributable to a lack of compatibility at that time, an internal 'flare up' resulting in pent-up anger and aggression being expressed and directed at each other. This is a common occurrence that can be well controlled once an understanding is reached by each partner, so that not only do they know when to give the other some breathing space, but they are also able to control their own reactions so as not to fuel the fire.

Relationships are about understanding and friendship, and how you decide to employ the information that a compatibility exercise can reveal is very much up to you. Guidelines have been established in this book to help you along but experimentation will ultimately lead you to adopt the most natural and comfortable approach for you.

During the course of this book most of the references to the effects of biorhythm take into account a varying number of external influences, such as outside pressure or involvement in a potentially life-threatening situation. It is important to be aware that the outside world and its effects on you will almost always affect you and your biorhythm in different ways. If you are low in your emotional cycle then the negative effects that this period could have on you would almost certainly be diminished if you discovered that you had just won a luxury house in a competition as the effects of biorhythm are often subtle and can be overridden in certain circumstances.

EXTERNAL INFLUENCES

Of course, our bodies are also susceptible to external influences. Biorhythm will operate with a higher degree of predictability if your body functions are operating at around their normal level. Things that need to be taken into account are factors such as levels of alcohol, lack of sleep and any health disorders. These factors will have a bearing on biorhythm's level of effectiveness, either by diminishing or increasing the perceived effects depending on the circumstances.

It is also possible actually to let biorhythm adversely influence you in some areas, as the psychological effect of knowing that you are going through a bad biorhythm condition can lead to a reduced ability to carry out normal activities that are well within your capability. It is important to define what biorhythm will alter within your own performance levels and to not let the science put you off any activities which would not normally be affected by a poor biorhythm condition. As you become acquainted with the science you will hopefully develop a certain degree of immunity to some areas of biorhythm activity because of your increased awareness of the potential hazards that are created, especially during critical days. This is the essence of applying biorhythm, to improve performance and harmony within your life. The key to this objective is to understand how to deal with, and adjust to, the many changing conditions that are operating within your physical, emotional and intellectual cycles.

THE BIORHYTHM CALCULATOR

This chapter contains the tables that you require to set your biorhythm calculator. The biorhythm calculator is set at the start of any month and has to be reset every month. The calendar sheet that comes with this system contains a universal 31-day format and can be used for all months. There are only three tables that you will have to use to set your curves. As you will know from the section in Chapter 2 that deals with the mathematical principles of the science, it is necessary to establish how many days you have been alive up to the day in question in order to calculate your biorhythm positions. Once you have established the total number of days, the calculation for *each* cycle is to divide that total by the cycle length to establish the remainder – which indicates how many days you are into the cycle for the day in question. The tables in this chapter have already calculated these remainders for you so there is no need for this laborious exercise; all you will be doing is adding the figures from three of the tables together to establish the positions that you will need to place each of the curve overlays at the start of the month.

If you examine the curve overlays you will notice that they are colour coordinated: blue represents the physical cycle; red is the emotional cycle and yellow is the intellectual cycle. Each of the curve overlays also has a series of numbers printed on it, which represent the total of the addition that you will have to carry out to determine where to position the overlay at the start of a month. As you will see from the diagram later in this chapter there are three sets of numbers placed in a collection of line up boxes on

THE TRANSPARENT CURVE OVERLAYS

the curve overlays. This is because the result of your addition from the three sets of tables may exceed the length of the cycle that you are setting, and so the calibration scales contain all the possible results. For example in the case of the intellectual scale you will see that all numbers from 0 to 96 are included. All the sets of numbers in each of the boxes are mathematically equivalent when related to the setting of the overlays, and this factor removes the need for you do any further calculations once you have added all the remainders from the three tables. If this sounds very confusing don't worry because a clear and simple example will demonstrate just how easy this technique is.

SETTING UP YOUR CHART

Please read fully the instructions and the working example before positioning any of the curves.

1   Using Table A on pages 137 and 138, look down the left hand column until you find your birth year.

2   Read across to the forecast year for which you wish to set your chart and select the numbers in the P, E and I column.

3   If you were born in a leap year (leap years are highlighted with white numbers in black boxes in the left hand column of Table A) go to Table C on page 140. Otherwise go to Table B on page 139.

4   Find your birthday in the appropriate Table (B or C) and select the numbers in the P, E and I column.

5   Add together the two sets of P numbers, the two sets of E numbers and the two sets of I numbers from steps 2 and 4.

6   You now have the master numbers that indicate the correct

curve overlay positions for the month of January in your forecast year. These numbers should be recorded because you will refer to them when setting up subsequent months.

7 To set up your chart for February and onwards you will have to refer to Table D, or Table E if the forecast year is a leap year. Both of these tables are on page 141. Using the correct Table find the month that you require and select the P, E and I numbers. Simply add the P number to your master P number to establish your correct physical curve overlay position for the month in question. Repeat the exercise for both the emotional and intellectual cycles.

Working Example: *d.o.b. 23 December 1962 Forecast date February 1991*

Numbers in Table A	P =15	E = 7	I = 30
Numbers in Table B	P =9	E = 9	I = 9
Master Numbers are:	P = 24	E = 16	I = 39
Numbers In Table D	P =8	E = 3	I = 31
Curve Overlay Positions	P = 32	E = 19	I =70

The diagram on page 136 indicates the intellectual curve overlay position for the working example featured.

Attach the adhesive pads to the back of the curves to hold the overlays once they are positioned (these pads are re-useable). Always place the overlays in the following order:

Before You Position The Curves

1 Physical curve
2 Emotional curve
3 Intellectual curve

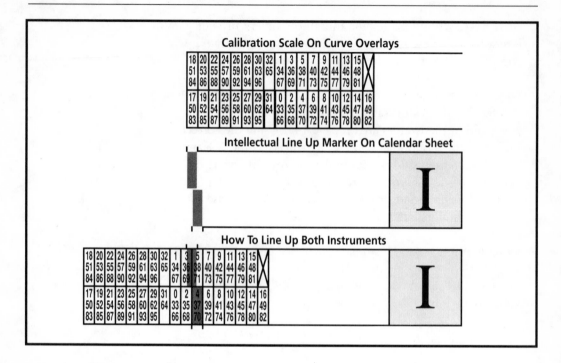

Curve Overlay Alignment Diagram

To check that you have got the technique correct it might be wise to try and set up an example from the celebrity biorhythm section. If you match the biorhythm patterns exactly then you are definitely following the instructions correctly.

Once you have set up the curves a number of times you will find that this technique will become straightforward, but a little care should be taken to ensure that you place the overlays as exactly as possible because it is important to make sure that all the curves are positioned correctly relative to each other. The line-up method that is employed is extremely accurate and simply requires a steady hand.

FORECAST YEAR																																				
	1989			1990			1991			1992			1993			1994			1995			1996			1997			1998			1999			2000		
Year of birth	P	E	I	P	E	I	P	E	I	P	E	I	P	E	I	P	E	I	P	E	I	P	E	I	P	E	I	P	E	I	P	E	I	P	E	I
1942	12	2	5	9	3	7	6	4	9	3	5	11	1	7	14	21	8	16	18	9	18	15	10	20	13	12	23	10	13	25	7	14	27	4	15	29
1941	9	3	7	6	4	9	3	5	11	0	6	13	21	8	16	18	9	18	15	10	20	12	11	22	10	13	25	7	14	27	4	15	29	1	16	31
1940	6	4	9	3	5	11	0	6	13	20	7	15	18	9	18	15	10	20	12	11	22	9	12	24	7	14	27	4	15	29	1	16	31	21	17	0
1939	4	6	12	1	7	14	21	8	16	18	9	18	16	11	21	13	12	23	10	13	25	7	14	27	5	16	30	2	17	32	22	18	1	19	19	3
1938	1	7	14	21	8	16	18	9	18	15	10	20	13	12	23	10	13	25	7	14	27	4	15	29	2	17	32	22	18	1	19	19	3	16	20	5
1937	21	8	16	18	9	18	15	10	20	12	11	22	10	13	25	7	14	27	4	15	29	1	16	31	22	18	1	19	19	3	16	20	5	13	21	7
1936	18	9	18	15	10	20	12	11	22	9	12	24	7	14	27	4	15	29	1	16	31	21	17	0	19	19	3	16	20	5	13	21	7	10	22	9
1935	16	11	21	13	12	23	10	13	25	7	14	27	5	16	30	2	17	32	22	18	1	19	19	3	17	21	6	14	22	8	11	23	10	8	24	12
1934	13	12	23	10	13	25	7	14	27	4	15	29	2	17	32	22	18	1	19	19	3	16	20	5	14	22	8	11	23	10	8	24	12	5	25	14
1933	10	13	25	7	14	27	4	15	29	1	16	31	22	18	1	19	19	3	16	20	5	13	21	7	11	23	10	8	24	12	5	25	14	2	26	16
1932	7	14	27	4	15	29	1	16	31	21	17	0	19	19	3	16	20	5	13	21	7	10	22	9	8	24	12	5	25	14	2	26	16	22	27	18
1931	5	16	30	2	17	32	22	18	1	19	19	3	17	21	6	14	22	8	11	23	10	8	24	12	6	26	15	3	27	17	0	0	19	20	1	21
1930	2	17	32	22	18	1	19	19	3	16	20	5	14	22	8	11	23	10	8	24	12	5	25	14	3	27	17	0	0	19	20	1	21	17	2	23
1929	22	18	1	19	19	3	16	20	5	13	21	7	11	23	10	8	24	12	5	25	14	2	26	16	0	0	19	20	1	21	17	2	23	14	3	25
1928	19	19	3	16	20	5	13	21	7	10	22	9	8	24	12	5	25	14	2	26	16	22	27	18	20	1	21	17	2	23	14	3	25	11	4	27
1927	17	21	6	14	22	8	11	23	10	8	24	12	6	26	15	3	27	17	0	0	19	20	1	21	18	3	24	15	4	26	12	5	28	9	6	30
1926	14	22	8	11	23	10	8	24	12	5	25	14	3	27	17	0	0	19	20	1	21	17	2	23	15	4	26	12	5	28	9	6	30	6	7	32
1925	11	23	10	8	24	12	5	25	14	2	26	16	0	0	19	20	1	21	17	2	23	14	3	25	12	5	28	9	6	30	6	7	32	3	8	1
1924	8	24	12	5	25	14	2	26	16	22	27	18	20	1	21	17	2	23	14	3	25	11	4	27	9	6	30	6	7	32	3	8	1	0	9	3
1923	6	26	15	3	27	17	0	0	19	20	1	21	18	3	24	15	4	26	12	5	28	9	6	30	7	8	0	4	9	2	1	10	4	21	11	6
1922	3	27	17	0	0	19	20	1	21	17	2	23	15	4	26	12	5	28	9	6	30	6	7	32	4	9	2	1	10	4	21	11	6	18	12	8
1921	0	0	19	20	1	21	17	2	23	14	3	25	12	5	28	9	6	30	6	7	32	3	8	1	1	10	4	21	11	6	18	12	8	15	13	10
1920	20	1	21	17	2	23	14	3	25	11	4	27	9	6	30	6	7	32	3	8	1	0	9	3	21	11	6	18	12	8	15	13	10	12	14	12
1919	18	3	24	15	4	26	12	5	28	9	6	30	7	8	0	4	9	2	1	10	4	21	11	6	19	13	9	16	14	11	13	15	13	10	16	15
1918	15	4	26	12	5	28	9	6	30	6	7	32	4	9	2	1	10	4	21	11	6	18	12	8	16	14	11	13	15	13	10	16	15	7	17	17
1917	12	5	28	9	6	30	6	7	32	3	8	1	1	10	4	21	11	6	18	12	8	15	13	10	13	15	13	10	16	15	7	17	17	4	18	19
1916	9	6	30	6	7	32	3	8	1	0	9	3	21	11	6	18	12	8	15	13	10	12	14	12	10	16	15	7	17	17	4	18	19	1	19	21
1915	7	8	0	4	9	2	1	10	4	21	11	6	19	13	9	16	14	11	13	15	13	10	16	15	8	18	18	5	19	20	2	20	22	22	21	24
1914	4	9	2	1	10	4	21	11	6	18	12	8	16	14	11	13	15	13	10	16	15	7	17	17	5	19	20	2	20	22	22	21	24	19	22	26
1913	1	10	4	21	11	6	18	12	8	15	13	10	13	15	13	10	16	15	7	17	17	4	18	19	2	20	22	22	21	24	19	22	26	16	23	28
1912	21	11	6	18	12	8	15	13	10	12	14	12	10	16	15	7	17	17	4	18	19	1	19	21	22	21	24	19	22	26	16	23	28	13	24	30
1911	19	13	9	16	14	11	13	15	13	10	16	15	8	18	18	5	19	20	2	20	22	22	21	24	20	23	27	17	24	29	14	25	31	11	26	0
1910	16	14	11	13	15	13	10	16	15	7	17	17	5	19	20	2	20	22	22	21	24	19	22	26	17	24	29	14	25	31	11	26	0	8	27	2
1909	13	15	13	10	16	15	7	17	17	4	18	19	2	20	22	22	21	24	19	22	26	16	23	28	14	25	31	11	26	0	8	27	2	5	0	4
1908	10	16	15	7	17	17	4	18	19	1	19	21	22	21	24	19	22	26	16	23	28	13	24	30	11	26	0	8	27	2	5	0	4	2	1	6
1907	8	18	18	5	19	20	2	20	22	22	21	24	20	23	27	17	24	29	14	25	31	11	26	0	9	0	3	6	1	5	3	2	7	0	3	9
1906	5	19	20	2	20	22	22	21	24	19	22	26	17	24	29	14	25	31	11	26	0	8	27	2	6	1	5	3	2	7	0	3	9	20	4	11
1905	2	20	22	22	21	24	19	22	26	16	23	28	14	25	31	11	26	0	8	27	2	5	0	4	3	2	7	0	3	9	20	4	11	17	5	13
1904	22	21	24	19	22	26	16	23	28	13	24	30	11	26	0	8	27	2	5	0	4	2	1	6	0	3	9	20	4	11	17	5	13	14	6	15
1903	20	23	27	17	24	29	14	25	31	11	26	0	9	0	3	6	1	5	3	2	7	0	3	9	21	5	12	18	6	14	15	7	16	12	8	18
1902	17	24	29	14	25	31	11	26	0	8	27	2	6	1	5	3	2	7	0	3	9	20	4	11	18	6	14	15	7	16	12	8	18	9	9	20
1901	14	25	31	11	26	0	8	27	2	5	0	4	3	2	7	0	3	9	20	4	11	17	5	13	15	7	16	12	8	18	9	9	20	6	10	22
1900	11	26	0	8	27	2	5	0	4	2	1	6	0	3	9	20	4	11	17	5	13	14	6	15	12	8	18	9	9	20	6	10	22	3	11	24
1899	9	0	3	6	1	5	3	2	7	0	3	9	21	5	12	18	6	14	15	7	16	12	8	18	10	10	21	7	11	23	4	12	25	1	13	27
1898	6	1	5	3	2	7	0	3	9	20	4	11	18	6	14	15	7	16	12	8	18	9	9	20	7	11	23	4	12	25	1	13	27	21	14	29

Table A – Years 1943 to 1987

FORECAST YEAR

YEAR OF BIRTH	1989 P	E	I	1990 P	E	I	1991 P	E	I	1992 P	E	I	1993 P	E	I	1994 P	E	I	1995 P	E	I	1996 P	E	I	1997 P	E	I	1998 P	E	I	1999 P	E	I	2000 P	E	I
1987	21	2	3	18	3	5	15	4	7	12	5	9	10	7	12	7	8	14	4	9	16	1	10	18	22	12	21	19	13	23	16	14	25	13	15	27
1986	18	3	5	15	4	7	12	5	9	9	6	11	7	8	14	4	9	16	1	10	18	21	11	20	19	13	23	16	14	25	13	15	27	10	16	29
1985	15	4	7	12	5	9	9	6	11	6	7	13	4	9	16	1	10	18	21	11	20	18	12	22	16	14	25	13	15	27	10	16	29	7	17	31
1984	12	5	9	9	6	11	6	7	13	3	8	15	1	10	18	21	11	20	18	12	22	15	13	24	13	15	27	10	16	29	7	17	31	4	18	0
1983	10	7	12	7	8	14	4	9	16	1	10	18	22	12	21	19	13	23	16	14	25	13	15	27	11	17	30	8	18	32	5	19	1	2	20	3
1982	7	8	14	4	9	16	1	10	18	21	11	20	19	13	23	16	14	25	13	15	27	10	16	29	8	18	32	5	19	1	2	20	3	22	21	5
1981	4	9	16	1	10	18	21	11	20	18	12	22	16	14	25	13	15	27	10	16	29	7	17	31	5	19	1	2	20	3	22	21	5	19	22	7
1980	1	10	18	21	11	20	18	12	22	15	13	24	13	15	27	10	16	29	7	17	31	4	18	0	2	20	3	22	21	5	19	22	7	16	23	9
1979	22	12	21	19	13	23	16	14	25	13	15	27	11	17	30	8	18	32	5	19	1	2	20	3	0	22	6	20	23	8	17	24	10	14	25	12
1978	19	13	23	16	14	25	13	15	27	10	16	29	8	18	32	5	19	1	2	20	3	22	21	5	20	23	8	17	24	10	14	25	12	11	26	14
1977	16	14	25	13	15	27	10	16	29	7	17	31	5	19	1	2	20	3	22	21	5	19	22	7	17	24	10	14	25	12	11	26	14	8	27	16
1976	13	15	27	10	16	29	7	17	31	4	18	0	2	20	3	22	21	5	19	22	7	16	23	9	14	25	12	11	26	14	8	27	16	5	0	18
1975	11	17	30	8	18	32	5	19	1	2	20	3	0	22	6	20	23	8	17	24	10	14	25	12	12	27	15	9	0	17	6	1	19	3	2	21
1974	8	18	32	5	19	1	2	20	3	22	21	5	20	23	8	17	24	10	14	25	12	11	26	14	9	0	17	6	1	19	3	2	21	0	3	23
1973	5	19	1	2	20	3	22	21	5	19	22	7	17	24	10	14	25	12	11	26	14	8	27	16	6	1	19	3	2	21	0	3	23	20	4	25
1972	2	20	3	22	21	5	19	22	7	16	23	9	14	25	12	11	26	14	8	27	16	5	0	18	3	2	21	0	3	23	20	4	25	17	5	27
1971	0	22	6	20	23	8	17	24	10	14	25	12	12	27	15	9	0	17	6	1	19	3	2	21	1	4	24	21	5	26	18	6	28	15	7	30
1970	20	23	8	17	24	10	14	25	12	11	26	14	9	0	17	6	1	19	3	2	21	0	3	23	21	5	26	18	6	28	15	7	30	12	8	32
1969	17	24	10	14	25	12	11	26	14	8	27	16	6	1	19	3	2	21	0	3	23	20	4	25	18	6	28	15	7	30	12	8	32	9	9	1
1968	14	25	12	11	26	14	8	27	16	5	0	18	3	2	21	0	3	23	20	4	25	17	5	27	15	7	30	12	8	32	9	9	1	6	10	3
1967	12	27	15	9	0	17	6	1	19	3	2	21	1	4	24	21	5	26	18	6	28	15	7	30	13	9	0	10	10	2	7	11	4	4	12	6
1966	9	0	17	6	1	19	3	2	21	0	3	23	21	5	26	18	6	28	15	7	30	12	8	32	10	10	2	7	11	4	4	12	6	1	13	8
1965	6	1	19	3	2	21	0	3	23	20	4	25	18	6	28	15	7	30	12	8	32	9	9	1	7	11	4	4	12	6	1	13	8	21	14	10
1964	3	2	21	0	3	23	20	4	25	17	5	27	15	7	30	12	8	32	9	9	1	6	10	3	4	12	6	1	13	8	21	14	10	18	15	12
1963	1	4	24	21	5	26	18	6	28	15	7	30	13	9	0	10	10	2	7	11	4	4	12	6	2	14	9	22	15	11	19	16	13	16	17	15
1962	21	5	26	18	6	28	15	7	30	12	8	32	10	10	2	7	11	4	4	12	6	1	13	8	22	15	11	19	16	13	16	17	15	13	18	17
1961	18	6	28	15	7	30	12	8	32	9	9	1	7	11	4	4	12	6	1	13	8	21	14	10	19	16	13	16	17	15	13	18	17	10	19	19
1960	15	7	30	12	8	32	9	9	1	6	10	3	4	12	6	1	13	8	21	14	10	18	15	12	16	17	15	13	18	17	10	19	19	7	20	21
1959	13	9	0	10	10	2	7	11	4	4	12	6	2	14	9	22	15	11	19	16	13	16	17	15	14	19	18	11	20	20	8	21	22	5	22	24
1958	10	10	2	7	11	4	4	12	6	1	13	8	22	15	11	19	16	13	16	17	15	13	18	17	11	20	20	8	21	22	5	22	24	2	23	26
1957	7	11	4	4	12	6	1	13	8	21	14	10	19	16	13	16	17	15	13	18	17	10	19	19	8	21	22	5	22	24	2	23	26	22	24	28
1956	4	12	6	1	13	8	21	14	10	18	15	12	16	17	15	13	18	17	10	19	19	7	20	21	5	22	24	2	23	26	22	24	28	19	25	30
1955	2	14	9	22	15	11	19	16	13	16	17	15	14	19	18	11	20	20	8	21	22	5	22	24	3	24	27	0	25	29	20	26	31	17	27	0
1954	22	15	11	19	16	13	16	17	15	13	18	17	11	20	20	8	21	22	5	22	24	2	23	26	0	25	29	20	26	31	17	27	0	14	0	2
1953	19	16	13	16	17	15	13	18	17	10	19	19	8	21	22	5	22	24	2	23	26	22	24	28	20	26	31	17	27	0	14	0	2	11	1	4
1952	16	17	15	13	18	17	10	19	19	7	20	21	5	22	24	2	23	26	22	24	28	19	25	30	17	27	0	14	0	2	11	1	4	8	2	6
1951	14	19	18	11	20	20	8	21	22	5	22	24	3	24	27	0	25	29	20	26	31	17	27	0	15	1	3	12	2	5	9	3	7	6	4	9
1950	11	20	20	8	21	22	5	22	24	2	23	26	0	25	29	20	26	31	17	27	0	14	0	2	12	2	5	9	3	7	6	4	9	3	5	11
1949	8	21	22	5	22	24	2	23	26	22	24	28	20	26	31	17	27	0	14	0	2	11	1	4	9	3	7	6	4	9	3	5	11	0	6	13
1948	5	22	24	2	23	26	22	24	28	19	25	30	17	27	0	14	0	2	11	1	4	8	2	6	6	4	9	3	5	11	0	6	13	20	7	15
1947	3	24	27	0	25	29	20	26	31	17	27	0	15	1	3	12	2	5	9	3	7	6	4	9	4	6	12	1	7	14	21	8	16	18	9	18
1946	0	25	29	20	26	31	17	27	0	14	0	2	12	2	5	9	3	7	6	4	9	3	5	11	1	7	14	21	8	16	18	9	18	15	10	20
1945	20	26	31	17	27	0	14	0	2	11	1	4	9	3	7	6	4	9	3	5	11	0	6	13	21	8	16	18	9	18	15	10	20	12	11	22
1944	17	27	0	14	0	2	11	1	4	8	2	6	6	4	9	3	5	11	0	6	13	20	7	15	18	9	18	15	10	20	12	11	22	9	12	24
1943	15	1	3	12	2	5	9	3	7	6	4	9	4	6	12	1	7	14	21	8	16	18	9	18	16	11	21	13	12	23	10	13	25	7	14	27

Table A – Years 1943 to 1987 inc

	JAN			FEB			MAR			APR			MAY			JUN			JUL			AUG			SEP			OCT			NOV			DEC		
	P	E	I	P	E	I	P	E	I	P	E	I	P	E	I	P	E	I	P	E	I	P	E	I	P	E	I	P	E	I	P	E	I	P	E	I
1				12	26	4	7	26	9	22	23	11	15	21	14	7	18	16	0	16	19	15	13	21	7	10	23	0	8	26	15	5	28	8	3	31
2	19	0	1	11	25	3	6	25	8	21	22	10	14	20	13	6	17	15	22	15	18	14	12	20	6	9	22	22	7	25	14	4	27	7	2	30
3	18	27	0	10	24	2	5	24	7	20	21	9	13	19	12	5	16	14	21	14	17	13	11	19	5	8	21	21	6	24	13	3	26	6	1	29
4	17	26	32	9	23	1	4	23	6	19	20	8	12	18	11	4	15	13	20	13	16	12	10	18	4	7	20	20	5	23	12	2	25	5	0	28
5	16	25	31	8	22	0	3	22	5	18	19	7	11	17	10	3	14	12	19	12	15	11	9	17	3	6	19	19	4	22	11	1	24	4	27	27
6	15	24	30	7	21	32	2	21	4	17	18	6	10	16	9	2	13	11	18	11	14	10	8	16	2	5	18	18	3	21	10	0	23	3	26	26
7	14	23	29	6	20	31	1	20	3	16	17	5	9	15	8	1	12	10	17	10	13	9	7	15	1	4	17	17	2	20	9	27	22	2	25	25
8	13	22	28	5	19	30	0	19	2	15	16	4	8	14	7	0	11	9	16	9	12	8	6	14	0	3	16	16	1	19	8	26	21	1	24	24
9	12	21	27	4	18	29	22	18	1	14	15	3	7	13	6	22	10	8	15	8	11	7	5	13	22	2	15	15	0	18	7	25	20	0	23	23
10	11	20	26	3	17	28	21	17	0	13	14	2	6	12	5	21	9	7	14	7	10	6	4	12	21	1	14	14	27	17	6	24	19	22	22	22
11	10	19	25	2	16	27	20	16	32	12	13	1	5	11	4	20	8	6	13	6	9	5	3	11	20	0	13	13	26	16	5	23	18	21	21	21
12	9	18	24	1	15	26	19	15	31	11	12	0	4	10	3	19	7	5	12	5	8	4	2	10	19	27	12	12	25	15	4	22	17	20	20	20
13	8	17	23	0	14	25	18	14	30	10	11	32	3	9	2	18	6	4	11	4	7	3	1	9	18	26	11	11	24	14	3	21	16	19	19	19
14	7	16	22	22	13	24	17	13	29	9	10	31	2	8	1	17	5	3	10	3	6	2	0	8	17	25	10	10	23	13	2	20	15	18	18	18
15	6	15	21	21	12	23	16	12	28	8	9	30	1	7	0	16	4	2	9	2	5	1	27	7	16	24	9	9	22	12	1	19	14	17	17	17
16	5	14	20	20	11	22	15	11	27	7	8	29	0	6	32	15	3	1	8	1	4	0	26	6	15	23	8	8	21	11	0	18	13	16	16	16
17	4	13	19	19	10	21	14	10	26	6	7	28	22	5	31	14	2	0	7	0	3	22	25	5	14	22	7	7	20	10	22	17	12	15	15	15
18	3	12	18	18	9	20	13	9	25	5	6	27	21	4	30	13	1	32	6	27	2	21	24	4	13	21	6	6	19	9	21	16	11	14	14	14
19	2	11	17	17	8	19	12	8	24	4	5	26	20	3	29	12	0	31	5	26	1	20	23	3	12	20	5	5	18	8	20	15	10	13	13	13
20	1	10	16	16	7	18	11	7	23	3	4	25	19	2	28	11	27	30	4	25	0	19	22	2	11	19	4	4	17	7	19	14	9	12	12	12
21	0	9	15	15	6	17	10	6	22	2	3	24	18	1	27	10	26	29	3	24	32	18	21	1	10	18	3	3	16	6	18	13	8	11	11	11
22	22	8	14	14	5	16	9	5	21	1	2	23	17	0	26	9	25	28	2	23	31	17	20	0	9	17	2	2	15	5	17	12	7	10	10	10
23	21	7	13	13	4	15	8	4	20	0	1	22	16	27	25	8	24	27	1	22	30	16	19	32	8	16	1	1	14	4	16	11	6	9	9	9
24	20	6	12	12	3	14	7	3	19	22	0	21	15	26	24	7	23	26	0	21	29	15	18	31	7	15	0	0	13	3	15	10	5	8	8	8
25	19	5	11	11	2	13	6	2	18	21	27	20	14	25	23	6	22	25	22	20	28	14	17	30	6	14	32	22	12	2	14	9	4	7	7	7
26	18	4	10	10	1	12	5	1	17	20	26	19	13	24	22	5	21	24	21	19	27	13	16	29	5	13	31	21	11	1	13	8	3	6	6	6
27	17	3	9	9	0	11	4	0	16	19	25	18	12	23	21	4	20	23	20	18	26	12	15	28	4	12	30	20	10	0	12	7	2	5	5	5
28	16	2	8	8	27	10	3	27	15	18	24	17	11	22	20	3	19	22	19	17	25	11	14	27	3	11	29	19	9	32	11	6	1	4	4	4
29	15	1	7				2	26	14	17	23	16	10	21	19	2	18	21	18	16	24	10	13	26	2	10	28	18	8	31	10	5	0	3	3	3
30	14	0	6				1	25	13	16	22	15	9	20	18	1	17	20	17	15	23	9	12	25	1	9	27	17	7	30	9	4	32	2	2	2
31	13	27	5				0	24	12				8	19	17				16	14	22	8	11	24				16	6	29				1	1	1

Table B – Non Leap Year Birthday

	JAN P	E	I	FEB P	E	I	MAR P	E	I	APR P	E	I	MAY P	E	I	JUN P	E	I	JUL P	E	I	AUG P	E	I	SEP P	E	I	OCT P	E	I	NOV P	E	I	DEC P	E	I
1				13	27	5	7	26	9	22	23	11	15	21	14	7	18	16	0	16	19	15	13	21	7	10	23	0	8	26	15	5	28	8	3	31
2	20	1	2	12	26	4	6	25	8	21	22	10	14	20	13	6	17	15	22	15	18	14	12	20	6	9	22	22	7	25	14	4	27	7	2	30
3	19	0	1	11	25	3	5	24	7	20	21	9	13	19	12	5	16	14	21	14	17	13	11	19	5	8	21	21	6	24	13	3	26	6	1	29
4	18	27	0	10	24	2	4	23	6	19	20	8	12	18	11	4	15	13	20	13	16	12	10	18	4	7	20	20	5	23	12	2	25	5	0	28
5	17	26	32	9	23	1	3	22	5	18	19	7	11	17	10	3	14	12	19	12	15	11	9	17	3	6	19	19	4	22	11	1	24	4	27	27
6	16	25	31	8	22	0	2	21	4	17	18	6	10	16	9	2	13	11	18	11	14	10	8	16	2	5	18	18	3	21	10	0	23	3	26	26
7	15	24	30	7	21	32	1	20	3	16	17	5	9	15	8	1	12	10	17	10	13	9	7	15	1	4	17	17	2	20	9	27	22	2	25	25
8	14	23	29	6	20	31	0	19	2	15	16	4	8	14	7	0	11	9	16	9	12	8	6	14	0	3	16	16	1	19	8	26	21	1	24	24
9	13	22	28	5	19	30	22	18	1	14	15	3	7	13	6	22	10	8	15	8	11	7	5	13	22	2	15	15	0	18	7	25	20	0	23	23
10	12	21	27	4	18	29	21	17	0	13	14	2	6	12	5	21	9	7	14	7	10	6	4	12	21	1	14	14	27	17	6	24	19	22	22	22
11	11	20	26	3	17	28	20	16	32	12	13	1	5	11	4	20	8	6	13	6	9	5	3	11	20	0	13	13	26	16	5	23	18	21	21	21
12	10	19	25	2	16	27	19	15	31	11	12	0	4	10	3	19	7	5	12	5	8	4	2	10	19	27	12	12	25	15	4	22	17	20	20	20
13	9	18	24	1	15	26	18	14	30	10	11	32	3	9	2	18	6	4	11	4	7	3	1	9	18	26	11	11	24	14	3	21	16	19	19	19
14	8	17	23	0	14	25	17	13	29	9	10	31	2	8	1	17	5	3	10	3	6	2	0	8	17	25	10	10	23	13	2	20	15	18	18	18
15	7	16	22	22	13	24	16	12	28	8	9	30	1	7	0	16	4	2	9	2	5	1	27	7	16	24	9	9	22	12	1	19	14	17	17	17
16	6	15	21	21	12	23	15	11	27	7	8	29	0	6	32	15	3	1	8	1	4	0	26	6	15	23	8	8	21	11	0	18	13	16	16	16
17	5	14	20	20	11	22	14	10	26	6	7	28	22	5	31	14	2	0	7	0	3	22	25	5	14	22	7	7	20	10	22	17	12	15	15	15
18	4	13	19	19	10	21	13	9	25	5	6	27	21	4	30	13	1	32	6	27	2	21	24	4	13	21	6	6	19	9	21	16	11	14	14	14
19	3	12	18	18	9	20	12	8	24	4	5	26	20	3	29	12	0	31	5	26	1	20	23	3	12	20	5	5	18	8	20	15	10	13	13	13
20	2	11	17	17	8	19	11	7	23	3	4	25	19	2	28	11	27	30	4	25	0	19	22	2	11	19	4	4	17	7	19	14	9	12	12	12
21	1	10	16	16	7	18	10	6	22	2	3	24	18	1	27	10	26	29	3	24	32	18	21	1	10	18	3	3	16	6	18	13	8	11	11	11
22	0	9	15	15	6	17	9	5	21	1	2	23	17	0	26	9	25	28	2	23	31	17	20	0	9	17	2	2	15	5	17	12	7	10	10	10
23	22	8	14	14	5	16	8	4	20	0	1	22	16	27	25	8	24	27	1	22	30	16	19	32	8	16	1	1	14	4	16	11	6	9	9	9
24	21	7	13	13	4	15	7	3	19	22	0	21	15	26	24	7	23	26	0	21	29	15	18	31	7	15	0	0	13	3	15	10	5	8	8	8
25	20	6	12	12	3	14	6	2	18	21	27	20	14	25	23	6	22	25	22	20	28	14	17	30	6	14	32	22	12	2	14	9	4	7	7	7
26	19	5	11	11	2	13	5	1	17	20	26	19	13	24	22	5	21	24	21	19	27	13	16	29	5	13	31	21	11	1	13	8	3	6	6	6
27	18	4	10	10	1	12	4	0	16	19	25	18	12	23	21	4	20	23	20	18	26	12	15	28	4	12	30	20	10	0	12	7	2	5	5	5
28	17	3	9	9	0	11	3	27	15	18	24	17	11	22	20	3	19	22	19	17	25	11	14	27	3	11	29	19	9	32	11	6	1	4	4	4
29	16	2	8	8	27	10	2	26	14	17	23	16	10	21	19	2	18	21	18	16	24	10	13	26	2	10	28	18	8	31	10	5	0	3	3	3
30	15	1	7				1	25	13	16	22	15	9	20	18	1	17	20	17	15	23	9	12	25	1	9	27	17	7	30	9	4	32	2	2	2
31	14	0	6				0	24	12				8	19	17				16	14	22	8	11	24				16	6	29				1	1	1

Table C – Leap Year Birthday

	P	E	I
February	8	3	31
March	13	3	26
April	21	6	24
May	5	8	21
June	13	11	19
July	20	13	16
August	5	16	14
September	13	19	12
October	20	21	9
November	5	24	7
December	12	26	4

Table D – Non Leap Forecast Year

	P	E	I
February	8	3	31
March	14	4	27
April	22	7	25
May	6	9	22
June	14	12	20
July	21	14	17
August	6	17	15
September	14	20	13
October	21	22	10
November	6	25	8
December	13	27	5

Table E – Leap Forecast Year

INDEX

The Biorhythm Calculator

PHYSICAL CURVE LINE UP   **P**

EMOTIONAL CURVE LINE UP   **E**

UNIVERSAL 31 DAY CALENDAR

+

C

−

| 1 | 2 | 3 | 4 | 5 | 6 | 7 | 8 | 9 | 10 | 11 | 12 | 13 | 14 | 15 | 16 | 17 | 18 | 19 | 20 | 21 | 22 | 23 | 24 | 25 | 26 | 27 | 28 | 29 | 30 | 31 |

INTELLECTUAL CURVE LINE UP   **I**